DICKENS

and

the Parent-Child Relationship

Dickens and his daughters
(left) Mamie and (right) Katey

DICKENS
and
the Parent-Child
Relationship

Arthur A. Adrian

OHIO UNIVERSITY PRESS
ATHENS, OHIO
LONDON

Library of Congress Cataloging in Publication Data

Adrian, Arthur., 1906–
    Dickens and the parent-child relationship.

    Bibliography: p.
    Includes index.
    1. Dickens, Charles, 1812–1870—Political and social views.
2. Parent and child in literature. 3. Parents in literature. 4.
Children in literature. 5. Child abuse in literature. 6. Family in
literature. I. Title.
PR4592.P34A37   1984   823'.8   83-19505
ISBN 0-8214-0735-X

To the memory of my parents

Peter Paul and Helena Harms Adrian

Contents

PART ONE

"A Fond Parent to Every Child of My Fancy"

PART TWO

A Nation's Glory, or a Nation's Shame?

Illustrations

Abbreviations in the Text

For convenience, because I own the *Gadshill Edition of the Works of Charles Dickens* (34 vols. edited by Andrew Lang, London: Chapman and Hall, 1897–1899), I have used it throughout in quoting from the novels. Because of their frequency, especially in Part Two, references to Dickens's writings are identified in the text, generally by abbreviated title, section, and/or chapter.

BR	*Barnaby Rudge*
BH	*Bleak House*
DC	*David Copperfield*
DS	*Dombey and Son*
GE	*Great Expectations*
HT	*Hard Times*
HW	*Household Words*
LD	*Little Dorrit*
MC	*Martin Chuzzlewit*
ED	*The Mystery of Edwin Drood*
NN	*Nicholas Nickleby*
OCS	*The Old Curiosity Shop*
OT	*Oliver Twist*
OMF	*Our Mutual Friend*
TTC	*A Tale of Two Cities*
UT	*The Uncommercial Traveller*

Preface

Although the subject of parent-child relations is important, at times almost obsessive, in Dickens, it has been dealt with only incidentally by biographers and critics. A full-scale discussion that focuses on this one aspect of his work is, surely, long overdue. Such is the following two-part study.

The first half, historical and biographical, reviews the treatment of children in nineteenth-century England and summarizes Dickens's relations with his parents and his own children. The second half of the book shows how Dickens used his familiarity with contemporary conditions and his personal background for fictional and artistic purposes. Specifically, it examines four recurring patterns of parent-child relations in his major novels. These involve (1) orphans who are left to the mercy of surrogate parents, (2) unwanted or ignored children who are hurt by unfeeling or indifferent parents, (3) children who have been misguided or corrupted by their parents, and (4) children who have been exploited by unprincipled or ineffectual parents to assume family responsibilities. Although these patterns do not cover all phases of the parent-child relationship in Dickens, they recur so frequently that they contribute substantially to the structural unity of the novels. They serve, moreover, as a basis for much of the social and political criticism in Dickens's works.

Because the inclusion of all the novels and every example to illustrate the recurring patterns could only be repetitive, I have been selective in my choice of representative situations. Equally persuasive conclusions could be drawn from works and examples not considered, but little would be gained from further amplification of points already established.

By bringing together fragmentary materials from a variety of sources, my study is actually a synthesis that focuses for the first time on a hitherto neglected topic. It is intended as another approach to the reading of Dickens's novels.

Acknowledgments

The following have directed me to valuable sources of information: Professor K. J. Fielding, Miss Katherine Longley, and Professor George Albee. Miss Marjorie Pillers, formerly curator of the Dickens House Museum in London, assembled the Dickens family pictures for me and called my attention to other useful materials at the Dickens House. The Department of Manuscripts of the British Library allowed me to transcribe the Katey Dickens Perugini letters to George Bernard Shaw in its collections, and Mrs. F. P. Kenyon, the copyright holder, gave me permission to quote excerpts. At the Eastgate House Museum, Rochester, England, I had access to unpublished documents and newspaper clippings relating to the Dickens family. Miss Ruth Hadlow, director of Children's Services, Cleveland Public Library, and Mr. Elmer Newman, reference librarian, Case Western Reserve University, Cleveland, directed me to the illustrations used in my opening chapter. Mrs. Susan Hanson, in charge of Special Collections, Case Western Reserve University, helped me to assemble the Nonesuch reproductions of the original illustrations of Dickens's novels, and also made other rare books available.

Professor Emeritus C. K. Hyder, University of Kansas, Lawrence, read an early draft of my book and suggested some important corrections and revisions. As with my previous books, my wife, Vonna Hicks Adrian, has again been my severest and most helpful critic. There is hardly a page that has not had the benefit of her revisions, both in style and content.

I must also acknowledge my indebtedness to the late Lloyd Paul Coburn, who, under my direction, treated certain aspects of the Dickens parent-child relationship in his doctoral dissertation. We had hoped, ultimately, to collaborate on a fuller treatment of this topic. His untimely death left me to carry on alone. Although my book necessarily repeats much of his biographical material, it approaches the subject with greater focus on Dickens's major novels and is, essentially, a new treatment of his central thesis.

Again, as for my earlier books, the American Philosophical Society assisted me with grants that enabled me to travel in search of essential materials. Without this assistance I should have missed some hitherto neglected sources. A sabbatical leave of absence from Case Western Reserve University allowed me to begin my project a few years before I retired in 1974.

Two of my chapters have appeared in condensed versions: chapter 3 in *Victorian Literature and Society: Essays Presented to Richard D. Altick* (Columbus: The Ohio State University Press, 1983) and chapter 8 in *The Dickensian*, LXVII (January 1971), 3–11.

I am indebted to the Trustees of the Dickens Fellowship for permission to include among my illustrations a selection of Dickens family portraits in the Dickens House collection. A and C Black (Publishers) Limited, 35 Bedford Row, London, have kindly allowed me to reproduce illustrations from pp. 315 and 317 of R. J. Unstead's *Looking at History* for my Figures 1 and 2.

Part One

"A Fond Parent to Every Child of My Fancy"

"It will be easily believed that I am a fond parent to every child of my fancy, and that no one can ever love that family as dearly as I love them."

Preface to David Copperfield

Chapter 1

The Little World of Children

"In the little world in which children have their existence, whosoever brings them up, there is nothing so finely perceived and so finely felt, as injustice," observes Pip on the way his sadistic sister has brought him up "by hand" (*GE*, Chap. 8). Subjected to periodic thumping, repeatedly put on a "mortifying and penitential" diet of bread crumbs and watered milk, and dismissed by adults as "naterally vicious," he has endured "perpetual conflict with injustice."

With this portrayal of Pip's boyhood Dickens was continuing into his final decade his crusade against the abuses inflicted on Victorian children. Identifying his own early suffering with theirs, he lashed out against a harsh society that victimized defenseless youngsters. From observation he knew only too well that many parents, regardless of their social status, repressed their children, denying them their individuality and their rights.

Especially stern was the discipline in Dissenting and Evangelical families, whose "gloomy theology," like that of the Murdstones, "made all children to be a swarm of little vipers" (*DC*, Chap. 4). Puritan by tradition and zealously reinforced by the Wesleyans, such discipline was based on the belief in original sin.[1] Considered innately depraved, for they had been conceived in sin, children must be subdued into complete submission; and parents, acting in God's place, should instruct them to be truthful, obedient, punctual, and respectful toward their elders. Dire threats and frequent corporal punishment were thought necessary to curb natural depravity. The mildest measures consisted of sending the culprit to bed with blinds drawn, taking away his toys, putting him on a diet of bread and water, or standing him in a corner with face to the wall. If these measures failed, cuffings and floggings usually produced the desired result. On occasion they also produced physical injury, such as deafness from repeated ear boxing. That disobedience, lying, or even loss of temper led to eternal damnation was impressed on tender minds by memory gems like the following from *The Peep of Day:*

Satan is glad when I am bad
And hopes that I with him shall lie
In fire and chains and dreadful pains.

"Take some time to speak a little to your children ... about their miserable condition by nature," James Hannay advises parents in *A Token for Children.* "They are not too little to die, nor too little to go to hell." Charles Kingsley was to show how such instruction could do irreparable damage to a child. In his *Alton Locke* the young Alton is never free of a guilty terror that he will wake one "morning in everlasting flames" (Chap. 1). But to the young John Ruskin the thought of these flames was even more terrifying, more real, for his zealous Evangelical mother once held his baby finger over a burning candle because he had been untruthful. The pain, she told him, was a mere foretaste of what liars must endure in eternal hell.

Less sensational but not less damaging were the tortures inflicted on children by meaningless religious instruction. Catechized until they could parrot the doctrine of original sin and redemption, all beyond their comprehension, they grasped neither the New Testament message nor Christian ethics. Strict observance of the Sabbath, moreover, caused them to view the church as a place of sourness and gloom. Such was the chapel Arthur Clennam was marched off to three times on Sunday, "morally handcuffed" like a "military deserter" (*LD*, Chap. 3). Aside from churchgoing, the Lord's Day, as strict Sabbatarians called it, was devoted only to reading such pious tracts as puzzled and frightened little Arthur by asking "why he was going to perdition?" A grown man, he was to vow, "How I hated that day!" (Chap. 3).

The sensitive child in such a narrowly religious home suffered guilt and shame. Like Pip he felt himself a sinner by the very fact of his birth. Such also would have been David Copperfield's fate, moreover, had he remained under the Murdstones' tutelage. Healthy ego thus diminished, many a child became unnaturally docile, subdued by the popular admonition, "Children, obey your parents in the Lord," for indeed obedience to parents was identical with obedience to God. In the partially autobiographical *The Way of All Flesh* Samuel Butler points up this Victorian emphasis by having Theobald Pontifex declare that no duty can be more important than that of "teaching a child to obey its parents in all things" (Chap. 20). No matter how questionable their own conduct, fathers and mothers were to be honored and loved. By analogy to the Crown, the head of the home must be respected and obeyed.

Common platitudes of the time, such as "Break a child's will or he will break you" and "spare the rod and spoil the child," reflected the attitude toward youthful independence. "The first signs of self-will must be carefully looked for, plucked out by the roots before they [have] time to grow," warns Theobald Pontifex (Chap. 20). There could be no relaxation of authority nor any undue show of tenderness. With characteristic and grimly humorous exaggeration, Dickens jabs at such harshness by having Susan Nipper, the otherwise good-natured young woman who watches over Florence Dombey, hold "that childhood like money, must be shaken and rattled and jostled about a good deal to keep it bright" (*DS*, Chap. 3).

A more subtle method of keeping young virtue bright imposed self-denial and sacrifice. In *The Years with Mother* Augustus Hare recounts how he was forced to "follow a code of penance" when he was not yet six. His appetite stimulated by tantalizing glimpses of a delicious pudding, he yearned to taste it. But before he could do so it was snatched away, and he was told to carry it to some poor person in the village. Such treatment was meant to prepare him for the sacrifices and disappointments of later years.

That children were generally regarded as small adults is borne out by typical drawings of the time, which show them as little men and women in clothes patterned on those of their elders. Even such a noted educator as Dr. Thomas Arnold considered "childishness in boys" to be a "growing fault," which he ascribed to the reading of "exciting books of amusement . . . [which] completely satisfy all the intellectual appetite of a boy, and leave him palled not only for his regular work . . . but for good literature of all sorts, even for history and poetry."[2]

Regarded as little adults, children enjoyed no coddling. Even in prosperous homes life could be spartan. Only the physically fit child survived, as physicians were called in for none but extreme cases. For mere constitutional delicacy a rigorous hardening process was preferred. Augustus Hare *(The Years with Mother)* tells how his Aunt Esther attempted to "subdue him" because of the chilblains which left open wounds on his hands and feet. Her remedial program required him to sleep on a straw pallet under a coarse blanket, in an uncarpeted and unheated room. When he rose to wash his face on winter mornings he often had to break the ice in his basin with a brass candlestick or his bare, bleeding hands. If he then came to breakfast silent from illness and misery, he was accused of bad temper. Even worse, he might be forced to eat sauerkraut because the smell nauseated him.

As for the child's intellect and imagination, they found little stimulation in such recommended juvenile literature as Mrs. Barbauld's *Evenings at Home* and *Hymns in Prose*. As for Thomas Day's *Sandford and Merton,* any perceptive young reader would have seen it as a too obvious attempt to improve his morals. Of all the didactic and moralistic books, however, none strove more blatantly to promote virtue than Mrs. Sherwood's *History of the Fairchild Family*. The children of this model family endure endless sermonizing; they meditate in dark closets on their minor transgressions; they view a corpse on the gallows in order to ponder the wages of sin at first hand. Nearer home, they receive a memorable lesson in disobedience when a playmate is burned to death while playing with fire. With instruction, warnings, reproof, books for children were designed primarily to improve their behavior.

If in their zeal to perform their duty such middle-class parents as the Fairchilds lacked all empathy with their children, parents in the lowest class of all, the London underworld, lacked all concept of responsibility toward their offspring. Themselves born into a world of dirt, vermin, hunger, disease, and crime, they could only pass on their heritage. Consequently children, legitimate or not, were abandoned by their mothers in workhouses and deserted by roving fathers seeking employment. Their origin unknown, they had neither family nor home. Dickens summed it up when he wrote of Miss Wade: "Put her in a room

Fig. 1.   A slum in Victorian London
(From *Looking at History* by R. J. Unstead)

in London here with any six people old enough to be her parents, and her parents may be there for anything she knows" (*LD*, II, 9). Roaming singly or in packs like young wolves, such abandoned vagrants became street Arabs, covered with rags, sheltering in arcades or empty cellars, huddled together for warmth, devouring spoiled fruit and vegetables thrown out of Covent Garden Market, begging, stealing, lying, cursing, plundering. The struggle to survive having made them destructive, brutish, cruel, they were hopeless outcasts, forced to keep moving. Of them William Blanchard Jerrold wrote in "Anybody's Child" (*HW*, 4 February 1854): "Anybody's Child is a little fiend, a social curse, a hypocrite, a liar, a thief." And in *The Haunted Man*, his last Christmas book, Dickens painted a poignant portrait of this "little fiend": "A face rounded and smoothed by some half-dozen years, but pinched and twisted by the experience of life. Bright eyes, but not youthful. Naked feet, beautiful in their childish delicacy,—ugly in blood and dirt that cracked upon them. A baby savage, a young monster, a child who had never been a child, a creature who might live to take the outward form of a man, but who, within, would live and perish a mere beast" (Chap. 1). Had the "State ... long ago made Somebody accountable for the child, and taken upon itself the duties of a parent," Dickens argues, "Anybody's Child, in lieu of the dreadful creature you recoil from, would now be a hopeful fellow, with the roses of youth upon his cheeks and the truth of happy childhood on his lips." Determined to overcome public apathy, Dickens never let up on his efforts to rescue the unwanted child. In *Our Mutual Friend*, his last completed novel, he still used irony to slash at society's neglect. "Show her a Christening," he comments on Pleasant Riderhood, the river scavenger's daughter, "and she saw a little heathen personage having quite a superfluous name bestowed upon it, inasmuch as it would be commonly addressed by some abusive epithet; which little personage was not in the least wanted by anybody, and would be shoved and banged out of everybody's way, until it should grow big enough to shove and bang" (I, 12).

Many such owners of "superfluous" names, if they survived the hazard of childhood, went to prison, were transported, or, if cunning enough to elude the law, persisted in crime and debauchery. In Henry Mayhew's *London Labour and the London Poor* a statistical study of 150 juvenile thieves shows that nearly half had been in prison before, many more than once, six at least twenty-four times. And some of the offenders were only eight years old! "They have been either untaught, mistaught, maltreated, neglected, regularly trained in vice, or fairly turned into the streets to shift for themselves. . . . The censure then," Mayhew argues, "is attributable to parents, or to those who fill the place of parents—the state, or society" (I, 418 ff.). But as the records of the period confirm all too clearly, the state, having shirked its responsibilities, dealt sternly with children when they became public offenders. Brutal floggings of imprisoned juveniles, even capital punishment, were not uncommon. The Crown Calendar for the Lincolnshire Lent Assizes, 1818, records, for example, that fifteen-year-old George Crow, charged "on suspicion" of having stolen three pounds and sixpence, was sentenced to death. Another minor, Thomas Young, seventeen, was executed for entering a home with intent to commit robbery. Though pre-Victorian, these examples are from the period of Dickens's boyhood and could be matched by similar instances of extreme cruelty to young offenders during the first half of the century.

How intimately Dickens was acquainted with juvenile crime, its background and punishment, is apparent in the barrister Jaggers's explanation of why he rescued the infant Estella by placing her with Miss Havisham: "Put the case that he often saw children solemnly tried at the criminal bar, where they were held up to be seen; put the case that he habitually knew of their being imprisoned, whipped, transported, neglected, cast out, qualified in all ways for the hangman, and growing up to be hanged. Put the case that pretty nigh all the children he saw in his daily business life, he had reason to look upon as so much spawn, to develop into the fish that were to come to his net—to be prosecuted, defended, foresworn, made orphans, bedeviled somehow" (*GE*, Chap. 51).

In this vicious environment parents not uncommonly exploited their own children, sending them into the streets to beg and steal, selling their clothes for drink, even encouraging elder daughters to take up prostitution and then living on their earnings. Promiscuity was common among the laboring poor, for many spurned the institution of marriage. With a succession of men using her home as a temporary residence, a mother might have children sired by different fathers. A typical incident is recounted by a contemporary sociologist. A small boy, appearing in school with a new pair of boots, was asked where he had got them. "One of my fathers give 'em to me, mistress," he answered, "the one that's at home this week."[3]

When minor children could not be cared for at home, the parish had the right to apprentice them to any trade. Here industry abused them, sending them off to any part of the country, often to the cotton mills for forced labor. Mere babes of six and seven worked as long as twelve hours daily, in stifling lint-filled rooms, always in danger of being mangled by unfenced machinery. Barely able to get back to the dormitories after a long day, they crawled into beds left still warm by the last shift, their only cover a rough horse blanket. Should the mill fail and have to close, the children were set adrift to roam the countryside and beg for food. Toward such inhumanity the world took the callous attitude typified by the following comment in the House of Commons: "It would be highly injurious to the public to put a stop to the binding of so many apprentices to the cotton manufacturers, as it must necessarily raise the price of labour and enhance the price of cotton goods."

Even worse was the oppression of the chimney sweeps. Orphans, bastards, and unwanted stepsons, they were generally sold to, or kidnapped by, a master sweep, who worked them many hours and spent little on their keep. There was no schedule of regular meals; the boys bolted down their food whenever they could find time; at night they slept on bags of soot in some damp cellar. Small for their age, they were driven up narrow flues, where they sometimes got stuck in the crook of a chimney. In such emergencies their masters would try to bring them down by building a fire under them. Knowing how mere children were brutalized by this vicious occupation, Dickens used irony, one of his most effective weapons, to attack the rapacious master sweeps responsible for the system. "Boys is wery obstinit, and wery lazy," declares Gamfield, "and there's nothink like a good hot blaze to make 'em come down with a run. It's humane too . . . acause, even if they've stuck in the chimbley, roasting their feet makes 'em struggle to hextricate theirselves" (*OT*, Chap. 3).

Of all child labor, that in the coal mine was the most appalling. As early as age eight or nine, sometimes even at four or six, boys and girls were harnessed to little trucks of coal which they drew in a crouching position through low passages to the larger openings. It is hardly necessary to point out that the mortality rate of such children was high. Almost totally deprived of fresh air and sunshine, unable to cleanse themselves of the coal dust embedded in their scalps and skin, they built no resistance to disease.

Of working children still at home, many were employed alongside their parents, to supplement meager incomes. Small and able to crawl under machinery, they were useful as piecers. While the adult workers lunched, the children cleaned machines, eating their own meal whenever they could snatch a few minutes. Their

Fig. 2.   A master chimney sweep and his "climbing boys" (From *Looking at History* by R. J. Unstead)

mortality rate was high, for they were often too tired near the end of their shift to avoid being caught in the unfenced machinery. Or, constantly breathing the lint-clogged air, they developed pulmonary disease.

To be sure, by prohibiting the employment of children under nine in cotton mills, by reducing the hours and improving the working conditions of others, and by making some provision for holidays and education, the Factory Act of 1833 was designed to correct abuses. Still, although working children were to benefit from this and subsequent legislation, factory inspection was often lax and laws were not strictly enforced. Generally an apathetic public ignored the plight of the little drudges whose cheap labor helped to ensure England's place as the world's wealthiest nation.

* * *

In all fairness it must be pointed out that the preceding summary of child oppression is based partly on highly selective literature, such as novels, autobiographies of sensitive artists, and studies of certain slum areas. It should not be concluded, therefore, that all children in the nineteenth century were oppressed or physically abused, for many parents enjoyed a happy relationship with their families. And even in homes where austerity and strict discipline had been the rule, some of the children later recalled their upbringing without bitterness, grateful for the training that had prepared them for the responsibilities of adulthood. Still, because Dickens saw even isolated instances of childhood abuse as intolerable and often, to arouse public indignation, exaggerated them in his attacks, they must be considered here as a basis for his condemnation of Victorian parents and society in general.

Assessing the deplorable state of England's children as it impressed him, Dickens assailed the apathy of his fellow citizens. "Where, in England," he asked in "Boys to Mend" (*HW*, 11 September 1852), "is the public institution for the prevention of crime among the neglected class of youth to whom it is not second but first Nature; who are born to nothing else, and bred to nothing else?" Of the politicians, members for "Verbosity," proud of their sheltered sons, he demanded: what if "your birthplace had been a filthy fever-breeding alley; had no voice of teacher ever sounded in your ears; had you been made a callous

Fig. 3.   Child "hurriers" at work in a mine

Fig. 4.   Girl dragging coal tubs
(From the report of the Parliamentary Commission on mines)

man by rubbing constantly against the hardest part of society; had your wife to be died of gin with which she sought to drown the despondent sense of a most wretched existence; had you gone to your daily work, leaving your boy in the pestiferous alley; what would he, what could he, have been!"

Dickens was concerned not only with families of the poor; his sympathies went out to children everywhere—to the lonely, the misunderstood, the mistreated, who were to be found in middle-class homes as well, where chilling piety masked selfish materialism. "I am the only child of parents who weighed, measured, and priced everything," reflects Arthur Clennam; "for whom what could not be weighed, measured, and priced, had no existence" (*LD*, I, 2). Whatever the social class, Dickens attributed childhood misery to "neglectful and unnatural parents," for whom he recommended "severe punishment" ("Small Beginnings," *HW*, 5 April 1851). Indeed, he seems to have covered parents in general with the blanket of his disapproval, for as early as 1844 he declared that he had observed them to be "invariably" selfish in their relations with their children.[4]

In his continuing crusade for the rights of children Dickens followed a tradition directly opposed to the Puritan and Wesleyan view of the child as inherently depraved. He upheld the cult of innocence, which stressed primeval goodness and natural piety. Deriving its inspiration from Rousseau, it was continued by Blake and Wordsworth, who saw children as seers, spiritually wiser than adults.[5] As will be shown later, Dickens would use one of his earliest novels to portray childish purity and inherent wisdom triumphing over worldly evil.

Pondering the injustices inflicted upon defenseless children, Dickens kept returning to his traumatic boyhood. Memories of that period fired his indignation against parents (and a society charged with parental responsibility) who either abandoned their children or exploited them for personal gain. In *The Haunted Man* he turned one of his fiercest attacks on those who tolerated such abuses: "There is not a father by whose side in his daily or nightly walk, these creatures walk; there is not a mother among all the ranks of loving mothers in this land; there is no one risen from the state of childhood, but shall be responsible in his or her degree for their enormity. There is not a country throughout the earth on which it would not bring a curse. There is no religion upon earth that it would not deny; there is no people upon earth it would not put to shame" (Chap. 3).

Spurred by poignant memories of his own childhood, Dickens used his art to launch a crusade that occupied him throughout his career. Though he was never to recover completely from the deep psychological wounds of his boyhood, he came to terms with his past by drawing upon memories of his own suffering for his efforts to reform the lot of nineteenth-century children. No subject so dominated his emotions, his thoughts, his utterances— epistolary, journalistic, or literary. For the genesis of his lifelong interest in parent-child relations it is necessary to consider the formative years of his boyhood.

Chapter 2

"A Child of Singular Abilities"

"No one had compassion enough on me, a child of singular abilities, quick, eager, delicate, and soon hurt, bodily or mentally . . . ."
                    Dickens's Autobiographical Fragment

In 1812 Portsmouth seethed with rumors of a possible French invasion, offset by reports of brilliant victories by the British fleet. It was the year Napoleon doomed his army by invading Russia; a year of famine, when wheat sold for 150 shillings a quarter (eight bushels) and salmon for a guinea a pound at the Billingsgate Market. Military and local social news was reported by the Portsmouth and Chichester *Advertiser,* which on 1 February noted that a "very splendid ball" attended by no fewer than two hundred had raised over 141 pounds for the widows and orphans of officers and men lost in recent naval engagements. Tradition has it that among the "distinguished naval and military characters present" were John Dickens, then a navy pay clerk in the Portsmouth office, and Elizabeth, his wife. A few days later, after another evening of dancing for this young couple, a notice appeared under the heading BIRTHS: "On Friday, at Mile-end Terrace, the lady of John Dickens, Esq. a son—"[1]

So it was a year of suffering and privation that marked the birth of the future novelist and social reformer, in a town he would later immortalize in *Nicholas Nickleby* as the home of Crummles' theatre. But he was not to remain there long. Sometime in 1814 his father was transferred to London and took his family with him. It was in that year that the Portsmouth and Chichester *Advertiser* carried the following announcement under the dateline "April 9th, Six P. M.": "A messenger is just arrived with Dis-

15

Fig. 5. John Dickens
(Dickens House)

Fig. 6.   Elizabeth Dickens
(Dickens House)

patches from Lord Cathheart, announcing BONAPARTE'S ABDICATION AND SURRENDER. He is to retire to the Isle of Elba, with a pension of £20,000." Less than a half century later Dickens would brilliantly recreate the period that had brought on the French Revolution and its bloody aftermath.

In 1817 another transfer took the Dickenses to Chatham. Here Charles enjoyed the only happy days of his childhood. Small for his age and rather delicate, he took little part in vigorous games, and buried himself in books. In later years Mary Weller, his nurse, recalled that he was "a terrible boy to read." His book held in his left hand, his wrist clasped with his right, he constantly moved up and down, all the while sucking his tongue. He also displayed considerable talent as a public performer whenever visitors came to see his parents, who would show him off by having him stand on a table to recite pieces or sing duets with his older sister, Fanny, in his sweet childish voice. Sometimes these performances took place before a larger audience at the Mitre Inn nearby.

Although Dickens was always to look on the Chatham years as the best part of his boyhood, they included episodes harrowing to the frail and highly impressionable child, not yet six. His easygoing parents either never questioned or ignored the conduct of their children's nurse, referred to in "Nurse's Stories" *(UT)* as Mercy, "though she showed me none." This nurse (actually Mary Weller) repeatedly made bedtime a terror with her blood-curdling tales, such as that of Captain Murderer, who married in a coach and twelve drawn by milk white horses with a single spot of red (said to signify bride's blood), brought out a golden rolling pin and silver pie board on "the day after their marriage," ordered his lady to make a pie crust, then cut off her head and baked her into a meat pie. Always preceded by the ominous filing of teeth, the Captain's subsequent marriages continued to supply him with meat pies until his last victim took a deadly poison just before losing her head. This time, after Murderer had "picked her last bone, ... he began to swell, and to turn blue, and to be all over spots, and to scream." When at last his bulk filled the room from wall to wall and floor to ceilng, he blew up "with a loud explosion."

The nurse had a repertoire of such stories, some punctuated

by dramatic refrains, whose approach little Charles always anticipated with sickening faintness. She would begin by "clawing the air with both hands, and uttering a long, low hollow groan." For additional horror she invented a "weird and glaring-eyed supernatural Tom," reputed to prowl about the world by night, sucking the breath of infants, with a "special thirst" for Charles's. With such tales lodged in the "dark corners" of his mind, the young boy's sleep was often broken by terrifying dreams. Yet Dickens's lifelong relish for horror would suggest that the nurse's tales fascinated as much as terrorized him. According to Angus Wilson the child "must have known" that he would not willingly have sacrificed "those nightmares which were to prove so fruitful to him."[2]

In other ways, too, the nurse's care was unsupervised. She moved, it seemed, in a large circle of married friends, whom she attended at lyings-in, frequently taking her young charges with her. One such occasion introduced Charles to death prematurely —to multiple death, in fact—for a woman had been delivered of four babies at a birth ("I am afraid to write five"). The little bodies, all dead and laid out on a clean cloth on a chest of drawers, reminded him of "Pigs' feet as they are usually displayed at a neat tripe-shop." While the customary hot caudle was being passed around, Charles was solicited for a contribution to a subscription. He refused, even though he had money with him. Accordingly he was given to understand that he "must dismiss all expectations of going to Heaven" ("Dullborough Town," *UT*). This rebuke could only have given him a sense of guilt.

Although much has been made of Dickens's early reading, it also lacked parental supervision—in this case hardly regrettable, though it would have been so judged by Victorian standards. Certainly the little library his father had collected offered glimpses of a worldly life beyond a child's experience or comprehension. What could he have made of Tom Jones's sexual escapades or Roderick Random's earthy language? As for *The Arabian Nights*, later to be a rich source of inspiration, would he not have puzzled over such a title as "The Tale of the First Eunuch"? Whatever his puzzlements, they were mental stretchings toward the adult world, precocious perhaps, but inevitable.

Less maturing because repressive was the Nonconformist

fanaticism to which the sensitive boy was subjected. Though as a rule his parents, nominally Church of England communicants, seem not to have taken religion seriously, they may have come under the influence of a Dissenting sect while in Chatham, where Charles attended a school run by the son of a Baptist minister. In any event, Dickens was never to forget how he had suffered as a captive of a fire-and-brimstone orator. "Carried off to platform assemblages at which no human child . . . could possibly keep its eyes open," he recalled in "The City of London Churches" *(UT)*, he had to pretend to listen to the ranting preacher: "I have sat under Boanerges when he has specifically addressed himself to us—us, the infants—and at this present writing I hear his lumbering jocularity (which never amused us, though we heartily pretended that it did), and I behold his big round face, and I look up the inside of his outstretched coat-sleeve as if it were a telescope with a stopper on, and I hate him with an unwholesome hatred for two hours." There can be little doubt that Dickens's distrust of Chapel clerics, to find expression in such pen portraits as Stiggins, Melchizedek Howler, and others, had its genesis here.

When John Dickens was again transferred to London in 1823, Charles's carefree boyhood came to an abrupt end. Waiting until the close of the school term before following the family, Charles took leave of Chatham, a shock he would never absorb. "Through all the years that have since passed," he was to confess in "Dullborough Town" *(UT)*, "have I ever lost the smell of the damp straw in which I was packed—like game—and forwarded, carriage paid, to Cross Keys, Wood-street, Cheapside, London? There was no other inside passenger, and I consumed my sandwiches in solitude and dreariness, and it rained hard all the way, and I thought life sloppier than I had expected to find it." He had left behind all that had introduced him to the world of beauty and wonder: the country walks, the afternoons on the banks of the Medway to watch the ships go out to sea, the leisurely strolls along Rochester High Street. Torn from scenes dear to him, he faced an uncertain future. Like Pip, who watched "the light mists . . . solemnly rising as if to show me the world," he, too, "had been so innocent there, and all beyond was so unknown and great . . ." *(GE,* Chap. 19).

He found nothing to reassure him in the immediate "unknown," his new home in Bayham Street, Camden Town, a house with four rooms, an attic, and a basement. An unfashionable suburb of London, then largely rural with open areas, it struck him as a "very uninteresting place of waste ground, and a miserable pool of water." Nettles and dockweeds grew in rank profusion. Abandoned shoes, bonnets, saucepans, and umbrellas littered the road. At the top of the street, signs advertised lodgings to let. From the washerwoman's house next door came the smell of soapsuds and the sounds of mangling.[3] By accumulating debts, John Dickens had been obliged to move his family to this shabby neighborhood. Even earlier, once in the suburb of Portsea, then again in Chatham, he had been forced to move to cheaper quarters. His failure to get along on his salary of £350 had often exasperated his mother, the former housekeeper of Crewe Hall, Chester. According to one source, she constantly harped upon her son John's "idleness and general incapacity."[4] (Only the latter charge was justified.)

Prone to ignore as long as possible any threats to their security, John and Elizabeth Dickens, like the Micawbers, eluded their creditors and enjoyed whatever advantages they could wangle from unsuspecting shopkeepers. Without much thought to the future they seized whatever pleasures the present had to offer. Typical of their reckless high spirits, the night before Charles was born Elizabeth Dickens went to a party with her husband and danced with vigorous abandon. (It must be remembered that Regency mores, unlike Victorian, could allow a pregnant woman this freedom.) Fortunately no complications resulted from this rashness, though the birth may have been hastened by a few hours.

Kept out of school, Charles "degenerated" (as he later reported in his Autobiographical Fragment) into cleaning his father's boots, running errands, and looking after his younger brothers and sisters. Brooding in the little back garret that overlooked "a wretched garden abutting on a squalid court," he longed to get back to school, to be "taught something anywhere!" With characteristic humor he would later allude to his neglected schooling in *Pickwick Papers,* where Tony Weller explains how he educated Sam: "I took a good deal o' pains with his edication, sir;

let him run in the streets when he was very young and shift for his-self. It's the only way to make a boy sharp, sir" (Chap. 20).

Because he had to dodge bill collectors, John Dickens either hid in his home or fled to places unknown and stayed away for days at a time. The jovial father, with whom Charles had begun to form the close ties normal for boys between the ages of five to ten; the pleasure-loving guide, who had always affected an air of gentility, now cowered somewhere in a corner of the attic or disappeared altogether while tradesmen banged at the door and loudly demanded to be paid.

While John Dickens eluded the bill collectors Charles made frequent trips to the pawnshop. His little bed, a brass coal scuttle, a roasting jack, a bird cage—all went for a fraction of their value. Though one can only speculate on how deeply the sale of his bed affected the young boy, today it is generally agreed that a child attaches great importance to this symbol of warmth and security. For Charles this loss may well have been an indication of parental rejection. The hardest wrench of all was the sale of the library of eighteenth-century novels. Through these books the boy in his garret had escaped into the world of romance.

Worse was to follow. Through a family connection (a James Lamert, the stepson of Mrs. Dickens's sister) arrangements were made for Charles to work in a blacking warehouse immediately after his twelfth birthday. In a damp, unheated, rat-infested building at 30 Hungerford Stairs, Strand, he pasted labels on bottles of Warren's bootblacking and neatly packaged them. Miserable at being "so easily cast away at such an age," he would later confide to his Autobiographical Fragment, he felt that no one had enough "compassion" on him, "a child of singular abilities, quick, eager, delicate, and soon hurt, bodily or mentally." His parents seemed "quite satisfied" and could hardly have been more so if he had been "twenty years of age, distinguished at a grammar-school, and going to Cambridge." A "little labouring hind," he had "no counsel, no encouragement, no consolation, no support, from any one." With burning conviction he would later write in *The Haunted Man* of parents "whose care soon ends, and whose duty is soon done; who cast their offspring loose, early, as birds do theirs; and, if they do well, claim the merit; and, if ill, the pity" (Chap. 1). One busy day his father visited the warehouse. "I saw [him] coming in at the door. . . ," Dickens recalled years later, "and I wondered how he could bear it."

This was a period of peril as well, for the twelve-year-old boy walked to work through such crime-infested districts as Seven Dials and St. Giles. "What wild visions of prodigies of wickedness, want, and beggary, arose in my mind out of that place!" he was to recall (*DC*, Chap. 11). "I know that, but for the mercy of God, I might easily have been . . . a little robber or a little vagabond." For, with his father finally having been arrested and sent to the Marshalsea Debtors' Prison on 20 February 1824, to be joined soon by Mrs. Dickens and the younger children, Charles was thrown entirely upon his own resources while he lived in lodgings in Camden Town and later in a back attic in Lant Street, where he moved to be nearer the Marshalsea. Nor had John Dickens's parting advice given him any comfort, though in future it may have stimulated his thrift: "He told me to take warning by the Marshalsea, and to observe that if a man had twenty pounds and spent nineteen shillings and sixpence, he would be happy, but that a shilling spent the other way would make him wretched" (*DC*, Chap. 11). Eking out an existence on his weekly six shillings, the boy occasionally spent too much on some tempting pudding, then had to go hungry until the next day. He was indeed a "not over-particularly-taken-care-of boy," as he confided to Washington Irving twenty-nine years later.[5] "When my thoughts go back now, to that slow agony of my youth," he would recall, "I wonder how much of the history I invented . . . hangs like a mist of fancy over well-remembered facts! When I tread the old ground, I do not wonder that I seem to see and pity, going on before me, an innocent boy, making his imaginative world out of such strange experiences and sordid things" (*DC*, Chap. 11).

Passing years blurred his anguished memory "of that life . . . fraught with such pain to me, with so much mental suffering and want of hope, that I have never had the courage even to examine how long I was doomed to lead it" (*DC*, Chap. 14). Although on 28 May, slightly more than three months after being committed, John Dickens was released from the Marshalsea under the Debtors' Insolvency Act, the humiliating employment at Warren's Blacking Warehouse was not to end immediately, a fact which his twelve-year-old son resented bitterly. Had not his father inherited £450 through Grandmother Dickens's will? As Angus Easson has shown, however, Charles as a mere boy would not have understood that "insolvent debtors were allowed goods to the value of £20 and no more; everything else went toward paying their creditors."[6] It was only when John Dickens quarreled with the family connection who had made the arrangements at Warren's that the harrowing warehouse experience ended abruptly. Even then Mrs. Dickens, who had every reason for questioning her impecunious husband's prospects, objected to losing her son's weekly wages. But John Dickens insisted that the boy go back to school and promptly enrolled him at Wellington House Academy, Mornington Place, Hampstead Road.

"I shall never forget, I never can forget," Charles was to confide to his Autobiographical Fragment, "that my mother was warm for my being sent back." Indeed, her willingness to sacrifice his education may have permanently soured her son's love for her. The fictional character he partially modeled on her, Mrs. Nickleby, is certainly portrayed as fatuous in the extreme. It may be reasonable to assume that his resentment colored a significant number of his other portraits of mothers: Mrs. Varden *(BR)*, Mrs. Skewton and Good Mrs. Brown *(DS)*, Mrs. Steerforth and Mrs. Heep *(DC)*, Mrs. Clennam *(LD)*, and Mrs. Wilfer *(OMF)*—all are unsatisfactory in meeting their maternal responsibilities, some even to the point of inflicting grave emotional damage.

Acutely sensitive because of his humiliating warehouse experience, Charles seems to have overreacted in his lifelong resentment of his mother's willingness to prolong his misery. Only a child, he would not have understood why his mother needed to be practical by supplementing her husband's uncertain income with her son's weekly wages. He understood only that it was his father who rescued him from the blacking warehouse and to whom he thus owed gratitude. As an adult, however, he needed to recall that he owed his first suitable employment to both parents, who found him a place as a junior clerk (he was only fifteen) with Ellis and Blackmore, a legal firm in Gray's Inn. Here he absorbed the atmosphere of the law courts, which were to become a compelling feature of his novels. Somewhat later he again entered employment which fostered his literary career, and again, however indirectly, through his mother's influence. It was her brother, John Henry Barrow, editor of the *Mirror of Parliament*, who gave him his journalistic start with this periodical. Later Barrow introduced him to Collier, the editor of the *Morning Chronicle*, who hired him as a reporter. The young man was now on his way. Though Dickens was aware of his mother's part in promoting these early experiences, and still more aware of how much they had contributed to his career, filial gratitude seems not to have colored his awareness.

Toward his father, whose ill management had brought on the family misfortunes, Dickens was more charitable. Although the improvident Micawber is drawn from him, John Dickens is nonetheless portrayed sympathetically. A blend of pathos and unconscious humor gives this master of grandiloquence his charm—as in his reference to London as "the arcana of the Modern Babylon" and to himself as "a shattered fragment of the Temple once called man" (*DC*, Chaps. 11 and 49). To little Charles such diction was inspiringly eloquent; to the adult Dickens it was comically grandiloquent. That his own creative imagination, and especially his turn for extravagant language, could be viewed as due in part to his father's example, he seems never to have acknowledged. To the Inimitable, as he would come to style himself, his genius was self-engendered, self-nourished. Although he did not openly credit his father as an inspiration for his own creativity, Dickens must always have been grateful to him for an early rescue from the blacking warehouse.

His humiliating drudgery lasted only a few months, but Dickens could never blot it from his memory. "How much I suffered," he recorded in his Autobiographical Fragment, "is . . . utterly beyond my power to tell. No man's imagination can overstep the reality." In the final decade of his life the past was still haunting him as he confided to John Forster how his "never to be forgotten misery . . . bred a certain shrinking sensitiveness in a certain ill-clad, ill-fed child, that I have found come back in this later time."[7]

His misery had been all the more acute because his sister Fanny had enjoyed the privileges of a scholarship student at the Royal Academy of Music in Tenterden Street while he was toiling as a "little hind" in the warehouse. "I could not bear to think of myself—beyond the reach of all such honourable emulation and success," he later explained in his Autobiographical Fragment. Watching Fanny receive a prize had been sheer torture: "The tears ran down my face. I felt as if my heart were rent. I prayed, when I went to bed that night, to be lifted out of the humiliation and neglect in which I was. I never had suffered so much before."

That his parents may have felt his plight keenly and may have guessed his despair while still helpless to relieve it, is obliquely suggested by Dickens's comment that in years to come neither of them ever made "the least allusion" to the agony of his months in the blacking warehouse. "From that hour until this, my father and mother have been stricken dumb upon it. I have never heard the least allusion to it, however far off and remote, from either of them." (Yet even if they had been callous at times, they could not have avoided full awareness after the publication of *David Copperfield*.) For all his knowledge of the human psyche Dickens was too closely involved to discern the possible implications of this telling silence: that his parents' trauma may have lain too deep for expression in words, an outlet open to their son. Apparently, though, Dickens never faced either of his parents with a direct reproach for the warehouse interlude. Denying himself this release, he could direct all the power of his private resentment into the public channel of his fiction, an effective means of arousing the national conscience.

There are those who consider Dickens's reaction to his unhappy boyhood overdrawn and sentimentalized, arguing that in the nineteenth century many boys were expected to be fully employed at the age of twelve. But Charles never thought of himself as an ordinary boy. It may be that the Barrows, the socially pretentious family on his mother's side, had given him an exalted idea of his heritage. Even his father's parents, through their employment at Crewe Hall (as steward and housekeeper), must have had the refined manners that intimacy with an aristocratic household would cultivate. Indeed, his grandmother had filled a highly respectable position, a fact Dickens recognized in making her the original of Mrs. Rouncewell, the admirable housekeeper in *Bleak House.* For her he must have felt a special affinity because she used to invent stories to tell her grandchildren. That he con-

sidered himself socially superior to his fellow workers at Warren's Blacking Warehouse is borne out by his Autobiographical
Fragment: "But I held some station at the blacking warehouse
too. . . . I never said to man or boy, how it was I came there. . . .
Though perfectly familiar with them, my conduct and manners
were different enough from theirs to place a space between us.
They, and the men, always spoke of me as 'the young gentleman.'"

Considering how conscious Dickens was of the social gap between himself and the other boys at Warren's, might his adult
mingling with lower-class children have been in atonement for
what he had come to recognize as his early snobbishness? Might
it not partially explain his years of dedicated service to the
Ragged Schools? Or why he repeatedly made friends with boys
from poor families, sometimes after only a chance meeting or
casual acquaintance? In *Billy the Cartwheeler* one W. Harrison
Culmer has left us a fascinating account of such a friendship.

Brought up in the London slums and educated at the Magdalen Ragged School, Culmer as a young boy met Dickens in 1861
and, until migrating to America with his family near the end of
the decade, enjoyed some memorable contacts with the novelist.
The occasion that brought the two together was the tenth anniversary observance of the 1851 Exhibition, at which 25,000
schoolchildren from nine to fourteen years of age were to
present a concert of national hymns and anthems before the
queen and other royal patrons. Chairman of the project was
Dickens, with whom, according to rumor, the plan to bring in the
children had originated. His insistence on including all the boys
from the Ragged Schools meant that "Billy" (Culmer), as a moni-
tor at Magdalen, would head twenty-five specially selected boys
from his school.

At their first meeting Dickens quizzed Billy on his reading,
drew out his reactions to characters in *Oliver Twist,* and asked
him questions about his family and his part-time jobs, all of them
low, menial tasks involving long hours under adverse conditions.
After several visits to the Culmer home Dickens arranged for
outings and picnics. The most memorable of these was a trip with
a group of boys from the slums by special stage coach to Windsor
Park, the host entertaining his young guests along the way with

lively anecdotes. Everything had been carefully planned, including a conducted tour of the Castle.

A two-week stay at Dickens's country home, Gad's Hill, introduced Billy to Harry and Edward, the two youngest members of the family, and to their aunt, Georgina Hogarth, whose efficiency in running the household impressed him. He had a room to himself with fresh flowers brought in daily. As Dickens's guest he had access to Cobham Park and joined him on rambles over the weekends. When Billy and his parents, converts to the Church of Latter-Day Saints, left for America to make a home in Utah, he brought with him some imperishable memories, which he recorded when, as an old man, he relived the happy events that had influenced him so profoundly in building a successful career.

What had hurt the young Dickens more than his humiliation was the bleak prospect of preparing for life without an education. Were his dramatic and creative talents to be stifled? Would there be no more public recitations, no more duets with Fanny? Had not Christopher Huffam, his godfather, called him a prodigy after watching his performance? And when would the "little drudge," the "labouring hind," have an opportunity to put into writing all the fancies that crowded his mind, all the closely observed sights that took on new life in his imagination?

That Charles was indeed creative he was to demonstrate when his warehouse servitude ended and he continued his schooling at Wellington House Academy. Here, on scraps of copybook paper, he produced *Our Observer*, to be circulated among his schoolmates on payment of marbles and pieces of slate pencil. His robust humor, which was to pervade much of his fiction, also manifested itself early. According to a fellow pupil, he would whisper comic remarks—dinner was waiting, the potatoes were spoiling—during the long, boring sermons at Seymour Street Chapel, convulsing the boys who sat near him. Once he persuaded some companions to pose as poor beggars and ask passing ladies for coins. Thus approached, one old woman furiously declared that she had no money for little beggars, at which Charles burst into laughter and led the boys in hasty retreat.[8]

Without playing down the unhappiness of Dickens's boyhood, one must in all fairness remember that the warehouse experience was of short duration. Before leaving Chatham, Charles had indeed enjoyed a privileged childhood. At home, before he attended school, his mother taught him to read and introduced him to the rudiments of Latin; both parents encouraged him to develop his talents by performing before visitors; and his father took him on frequent country walks, which sharpened his powers of observation, enormously useful to him later. Even the few months he endured at Warren's may have been fortunate in a sense, for they were to serve as a goad to creativity. "I know that all these things have worked together to make me what I am," he was to acknowledge eventually.[9] Without this background might he not have been just another Smollett? Ironically, his never-to-be-forgotten unhappiness was also to become the source of much of his mature power. Because of his father's detention at the Marshalsea, for instance, he was to return repeatedly to the prison theme. What would *Barnaby Rudge, David Copperfield, Little Dorrit, A Tale of Two Cities,* and *Great Expectations* have been without it?

Yet, precisely because Dickens the boy was sensitive, his relatively brief privations had more than ordinary impact. Having lost the security of his Chatham days, he came to see himself as a victim of a ruthless money ethic that ignored the sufferings of the poor. Gradually he enlarged his self-pity to embrace all those children whom an indifferent society condemned to lives of hunger, disease, and crime. The indignation fired by such social injustice would henceforth inspire his fiction and sustain an important thesis in each of his major novels.

Chapter 3

"Why Was I Ever a Father!"

"I can't get my hat on in consequence of the extent to which my hair stands on end at the costs and charges of these boys. Why was I ever a father!"

Dickens to George Dolby, 25 September 1868, Berg MS

In addition to shaping his social vision, Dickens's boyhood undoubtedly laid the foundation for his practices in bringing up his own children. As the head of a large family he had ample opportunity for testing his parental competence, without, however, always achieving the hoped-for results. Determined to spare his children the heartaches he had experienced as a not "over-particularly-taken care-of boy," he organized his home along principles that set it apart from the typically austere Victorian household.

It was during their early years that Dickens had the closest rapport with his children. He found babies irresistible. And they, even when strangers, seemed to sense his affection. "I have often seen mere babies," his daughter Mary (Mamie) has told us, "who would look at no other stranger present, put out their tiny arms to him with unbounded confidence, or place a small hand in his and trot away with him, quite proud and contented at having found such a companion." She adds that his manner with his own children, though sometimes sterner, did not inhibit them from going to him with their problems, however trivial, and that "in him they would always find unvarying justice and love."[1] During even his briefest absences from home he missed them. "I kiss almost all the children I encounter," he told his wife, "in remembrance of their sweet faces, and talk to all the mothers who carry them."[2]

In talking to his children, Dickens used a peculiar tone of voice

30

for each one. Even when not called by name, each knew exactly who was being addressed.[3] And in a characteristically playful mood their father gave each child a distinguishing nickname. Charles (Charley), the oldest was "Flaster Floby," a corruption of "Master Toby." Because of her gentle nature, Mamie was called "Mild Glo'ster." Katey, a great favorite, was "Lucifer Box" because of her occasional bursts of fiery temperament. Walter was "Young Skull" because of his high cheekbones. Francis Jeffrey was "Chicken Stalker"; Sydney, fascinated even in infancy by the sea, was "Ocean Spectre," sometimes shortened to "Hoshen Peck." Alfred Tennyson had two nicknames: "Sampson Brass" and "Skittles," from "something skittle-playing and public-housey in his countenance," explained Dickens. Henry Fielding (Harry), who was to prove the most dependable of the sons, was variously known as "The Jolly Postboy" and "The Comic Countryman." Edward, the youngest, bore the weight of seven syllables: "Plornishmaroontigoonter," shortened to "Plorn." Each of these names, Dickens told his brother-in-law, was pronounced with "a peculiar howl, which I shall have great pleasure in illustrating."[4]

The key to winning his children's confidence was Dickens's ability to be a child among them. His love of surprise, his dramatic rendering of comic songs, and his enjoyment of the ludicrous all appealed to the young. In any celebration, especially birthdays, he participated wholeheartedly. "Even if I had an engagement of the most particular kind," he wrote his daughter Mamie before her tenth birthday, "I should excuse myself from keeping it, so that I might have the pleasure of celebrating at home, and among my children, the day that gave me such a dear and good daughter as you."[5] Nothing, not even his illness, could prevent his surprising her. Once, unwell and unable to come down for her birthday, he sent for her, put his arms around her, kissed her, and wished her many happy returns of the day. Then, drawing a case from under his pillow, he presented her with a gold watch, the emerald back bearing her initials in enamel. When, after some speechless seconds, she was able to exclaim in delight, she turned to her father and met his tear-filled eyes.[6]

His love of surprise did not diminish as his children grew older. When in 1851 the family prepared to move to Tavistock House, he promised his daughters that they would have a better bedroom than they had ever had. But they were not to see their "gorgeous apartment" until all was in readiness. When the long-awaited day finally arrived, Dickens took his daughters on their first tour of inspection. Every detail had been planned according to his ideas of their needs and tastes: the flowered wall paper, the chintz-covered bedsteads, the toilet tables, the writing tables, and the easy chairs—all in pairs—nothing had been overlooked.[7] All this when English bedrooms were generally spartan in their furnishings! It would hardly have occurred to docile Mamie to wish she might have had a hand in this delightful project; to the younger but more independent Katey, the thought might have occurred.

As an entertainer Dickens charmed his children almost from their infancy. One child on each knee and the others gathered round his rocking chair (acquired on his first trip to America), he would sing them comic songs at bedtime. A special favorite, which told the story of an old man plagued with a cold and rheumatism, had to be rendered to the accompaniment of sneezes, coughs, and gestures. It was so popular that the small audience demanded repeated encores. Another favorite related the history of Guy Fawkes, "the prince of sinisters,/ Who once blew up the House of Lords,/ The King and all his ministers." Each stanza ended with a noisy refrain that charmed little ears: "Bow, wow, wow, wow, ri foldi riddi, oddy, bow, wow, wow."[8]

Each year, with the approach of Christmas, Dickens became once more a child among his children. "It is good to be children sometimes," he declared, "and never better than at Christmas, when its Mighty Founder was a child Himself."[9] Usually taking the whole week off before the holidays, he personally supervised the preparations: the special foods with their tantalizing aromas, the holly-decked walls, the invitations to house guests—all excited him. The day before Christmas, as long as the family lived in London, he would take his children to a toy shop in Holborn, where they were allowed to select their own gifts and any they wished to give their friends. Though it was often an hour or more before they could make up their minds, he never begrudged them the time.[10] At the Christmas feast, climaxed by the entry of the blazing plum pudding, resplendent on its holly-decked china platter, Dickens always delivered his Christmas blessing: "Reflect upon your blessings—of which every man has many—not on your past misfortunes, of which all men have some. Fill your glass again, with a merry face and a contented heart. Our life on it, but your Christmas shall be merry and your new year a happy one."[11]

Sometimes Dickens was so carried away by his childlike enthusiasm that he took over completely a project originally intended for one of his sons. Such was the case when he and Clarkson Stanfield set up a toy theatre, a specimen of Drury Lane, which had been bought for Charley. So fascinated were the two men by this project that the boy could only look on as they painted, cut, and gummed.[12]

Because Charley's birthday fell on Twelfth Night, the occasion called for elaborate parties. A magic lantern, conjuring tricks, games of blindman's buff, dancing—there was no limit to the hilarity. Always it was Dickens who dominated the scene. "I have made a tremendous hit with a conjuring apparatus," he told Angela Burdett-Coutts, the philanthropist who was Charley's godmother and always sent him a large cake on his birthday. Dickens reported winning great popularity with the small fry "after cooking a plum pudding in a hat, and producing a pocket handkerchief from a Wine Bottle."[13]

As soon as the younger children could participate in the activities, they were assigned roles in the amateur theatricals staged in the schoolroom at Tavistock House. Beginning with *Tom Thumb* in 1854, the performances soon became finished productions with the addition of adult actors from Dickens's experienced troupe of amateurs. Rehearsals were serious affairs, and all knew there must be no trifling. According to Charley, December became one "long rehearsal." Dickens took infinite pains to teach the children their parts, helping them individually to memorize their lines and directing their acting. Though always patient and understanding, he demanded each one's best efforts. "Do everything at your best," he would say of any undertaking. "I shall not mind if you do not succeed in what you are doing, so long as I feel sure that you have done your best." It was a principle to which he himself adhered. "I can truly assure you that I have taken as great pains with the smallest thing I have ever undertaken as with the biggest," he told his sons.[14]

For his two daughters he arranged dancing lessons almost as soon as they could walk. "I hope the dancing lessons will be a success," he wrote his wife during one of his absences from home. "Don't fail to let me know."[15] As the girls improved, he encouraged them by praising their gracefulness and skill. One winter, in preparation for the Twelfth Night party, he asked them to teach him the polka. Having spent hours learning the steps, all with great enthusiasm and to the accompaniment of much laughter, he woke up early next morning and tried unsuccessfully to recall them. Dark as it was, he leaped out of bed and, on the cold floor, practiced until the steps came back to him."[16]

From the outset the Dickens home was never without pets, today considered indispensable in helping children to develop responsibility. In the 1840s there was Grip the Raven, whose antics delighted everyone. He was succeeded in turn by two more ravens, one of whom swallowed keys and pecked invaders. Timber, a white spaniel, had come with the Dickenses from America in 1842 and accompanied them to Italy in 1844. At Gad's Hill near Rochester, Dickens's country home during his last decade, there was a veritable menagerie. Turk (a mastiff), Linda (a St. Bernard), Bumble (a Newfoundland), and Mrs. Bouncer (a Pomeranian named after a character in *Cox and Box*) all kept watch over the premises, inside and out. Wilhelmina, a cat, walked the lanes after her master like a dog. Dick, a goldfinch trained to draw his own water by means of a chain and cup, eventually rated a handsome tombstone with an epitaph by Dickens.[17] There was even a pony named Newman Noggs, after the character in *Nicholas Nickleby*.

A family project viewed with considerable pride took form in 1863, when Harry and three of his brothers organized a small newspaper to record the week's local events. Called the Gad's Hill *Gazette,* it began with one handwritten sheet, but eventually became four printed pages run off on a real printing press, the gift of W. H. Wills, Dickens's subeditor. At the peak of its success it had a hundred subscribers, who paid twopence a copy for news about the Dickens family and friends: about the Gad's Hill dinners ("served up in the same magnificent and costly manner as usual"), the games ("again resorted to, until eleven o'clock, when the visitors retired to their proper homes, and the residents to

Fig. 7.   Mrs. Bouncer, a Pomeranian, a household pet at
Gad's Hill Place
(Dickens House)

their beds"), the annual New Year's parties (at which "the usual formula was gone through" and the guests were "favoured with the chimes of the gong"), the amateur theatricals (staged by the Gad's Hill visitors and servants under Harry's direction at the Theatre Royal Club Room, with Dickens and the music critic Henry Chorley causing "incessant laughter" between the scenes), Charles Albert Fechter's gift of a Swiss chalet (now completed by his "furnishing it in a very handsome manner"), Marcus Stone's portrait of Katey ("very creditable to the artist"), and the Staplehurst railway accident (where "the courage and intrepidity of Mr. Dickens" saved the lives of fellow passengers). Still other newsworthy reports covered illnesses, travels, arrivals and departures, and village incidents.

That Dickens himself supplied some of the material for the *Gazette* is evident from a few pages of copy preserved in his handwriting. Usually he helped out when Harry, who eventually assumed sole responsibility for the paper, ran short of material. At such times he would contribute humorous letters with fictitious signatures to register a complaint and denounce the paper in one number, only to come out with a strong defense of the editorial policies, contents, and format in the next. Thus a letter signed "Zabez Skinner, the Skinnery, Flintshire" would be answered by "Blackberry Jones, the Jonery, Everyshire."

For all his love of fun, occasionally displayed in ludicrous antics, Dickens could be serious, even stern, especially in his demands for orderliness and punctuality. Some of his letters, as well as the reminiscences of his son Harry, tell of his daily inspection of the boys' rooms. "Nothing is allowed to be out of place," Dickens reported during the family's stay in Boulogne. "Each in his turn is appointed Keeper for the week, and I go out in solemn procession . . . three times a day, on a tour of inspection."[18] It was a standing joke among his children that "he must be personally acquainted with every nail in the house." According to Harry, "there was a parade from time to time to check the stains of grease and dirt which had accumulated on . . . clothing; and to one boy was allotted the task each week of collecting the sticks, balls and croquet and cricket materials." On outings or picnics each was charged with cleaning up; not a single scrap of paper or bit of waste ever escaped Dickens's sharp eye.[19]

About punctuality for meals or appointments Dickens was equally strict. One of his granddaughters has recalled an early experience at Gad's Hill. After some awkward moments at table, she ("Mekitty"), "the small observer in muslin pinafore," concluded that "somebody is late for dinner" and that "Venables" ["Venerables," a name Dickens preferred to "Grandfather"] does not like people to be late."[20] What punishment was meted out for breaking rules is not a matter of record, though in a letter to Landor (3 September 1853) Dickens mentioned having put the twelve-year-old Walter, "a very good boy," in solitary bathroom confinement for "terminating a dispute with a nurse by throwing a chair in her direction." Usually, however, Dickens's displeasure was a sufficient deterrent. At the same time he was quick to reward his children with special treats and prizes in recognition of neatness and promptness.

Always ready to give their small problems his sympathetic understanding, he encouraged his sons and daughters to come to him for advice. At no time would he snub them, intimidate them, make them feel foolish, however unreasonable their requests. Even as toddlers they were never to be frightened, never to be sent against their will into the dark. "If the fixed impression be of an object terrible to the child," Dickens maintained, "it will be (for want of reasoning upon) inseparable from great fear. Force the child at such a time, be Spartan with it, send it into the dark against its will, and you had better murder it."[21]

Never did the children feel their father's affection more deeply than during their illnesses. His presence in the sickroom eased their pain, quieted their raging fever, drove away their fear. "Quick, active, sensible, bright and cheery . . . ," Mamie would reminisce later, "he could seize the 'case' at once, knew exactly what to do, and do it."[22] At the sound of his footsteps the little heart would beat faster and the eyes brighten as his reassuring voice greeted the invalid. There was something magnetic in his touch, a "curious life-giving power," Anne Thackeray Ritchie called it, the combined tenderness of a woman and his own mysteriously dominant strength.[23]

To no part of his children's upbringing did Dickens devote more attention than to their education. Basically he was concerned that it should take into account their individual aptitudes.

To the headmasters of his sons' schools he wrote repeatedly about the boys' special interests, their specific weaknesses, and his own hopes for them. Charley, with his facility for languages, was encouraged to consolidate his French by attending the Parisian theatres. For learning the language in three months he was awarded a Geneva watch. After Eton, where his father visited him regularly to check on his progress and picnic with him and his friends, he went to Germany to learn the language because he had decided on a commercial career. The boys were to consider their education a preparation for a definite calling. When they showed little aptitude for academic pursuits, they were switched to practical training that would prepare them for their life's work.

Only one of the sons, Harry, attended a university. It was not that Dickens opposed higher education, but he had to be sure that the money would be spent wisely. Before sending Harry to Cambridge, he asked his headmaster whether the boy really had the "qualities and habits" necessary to marked success there. "I could by no means afford," he insisted, "to send a son to college who went there for any other purpose than to work hard, and to gain distinction."[24]

As for the daughters, though preparation for a career was not the object, Dickens engaged tutors for them and encouraged them to acquire fluency in French. He urged Mamie to develop her musical talent; Katey, because of her special aptitude for art, was enrolled in drawing lessons at Bedford College. In short, the education of his children was one of Dickens's major concerns.

At the same time he made certain that their instruction would not embrace opinions he could not approve of. Hence, as he told Angela Burdett-Coutts, he was writing a history of England for Charley, so that he might have "tender-hearted notions of War and Murder" and not fix his "affections on the wrong heros [sic], or see the bright side of Glory's sword and know nothing of the rusty one."[25] Published serially in *Household Words* at irregular intervals from January 1851 to September 1853, *A Child's History of England* can hardly be considered an impartial appraisal of England's monarchs. Henry VIII, for instance, is denounced as "one of the most detestable villains that ever drew breath," a "Royal pig," a "disgrace to human nature." Other rulers fare little better. James I is referred to as "his sowship"; James II is condemned as a "besotted blunderer" who tried to reestablish the Catholic religion in England; Charles II is dismissed as a "Merry Judas"; and Elizabeth deserves to be remembered as only "half as good as she has been made out." On political and historical matters Dickens was always forthright.

Equally definite were his ideas about the religious instruction his children should receive. Introduced as a boy to the rantings of a Dissenting preacher in Chatham, next door to his home in St. Mary's Terrace, he could not forget how he had been "caught in the palm of a female hand by the crown, . . . violently scrubbed from the neck to the roots of the hair as a purification for the Temple, and . . . carried off, . . . to be steamed like a potato in the unventilated breath of Boanerges Boiler and his congregation" ("City of London Churches," *UT*). (As already stated, Dickens's parents may have come under the influence of a Chapel sect while living in Chatham.) Because of his early conditioning, Dickens always opposed any form of worship which, in the words of Carlyle, had "its eye forever turned on its own navel" (*Past and Present,* II, 15). On spiritual matters he was decidedly reticent, refusing to cheapen religion by playing on the emotions. Though nominally an Anglican, he found more congenial the Unitarian worship, in whose chapels he took sittings at various times. Like the Unitarians, he did not believe in the virgin birth, nor did he subscribe to the Nicene creed.

For his younger children he vehemently opposed any instruction in religious mysteries which they could but "imperfectly understand." Nor would he tolerate "frequent references to the Almighty in small matters." Why should children be made to see God as "avenging and wrathful"? It was preposterous to believe that the Creator, who in His wisdom had made them children before they were men and women, would "punish them awfully for every venial offence" which was but a "necessary part" of their growing up. They were not to see God as a rigid judge or to be imbued with the fear of death. "If God be as rigid as they are told," Dickens maintained, "their fathers and mothers and three fourths of their relations and friends must be doomed to Eternal Perdition." Under no circumstances was anyone to use such terms as "Lamb of God" or impose "injudicious catechising" upon his children. Rather than have them subjected to "religious forms of restraint" in a house of worship, Dickens would have them acquire "the principles of religion from a contemplation of nature and all the goodness and beneficence of the Great Being who created it."[26]

In this spirit he wrote one of his prayers for them: "Pray God who has made everything and is so kind and merciful to everything he has made: pray God to bless my dear Papa and Mama, brothers and sisters, and all my relations and friends: make me a good little child and let me never be naughty and tell a lie, which is a mean and shameful thing. Make me kind to my nurses and servants and to all beggars and poor people and let me never be cruel to any dumb creature, for if I am cruel to anything, even to a poor little fly, you, who are so good, will never love me: and pray God to bless and preserve us all this night and for ever, for the sake of Jesus Christ, our Lord, Amen."[27] In permanently withdrawing God's love from the sinner, Dickens injects an unorthodox bit of theology here, at variance with his known belief. Could he have wished any child of his to come under this threat? Obviously, his zeal to point out the right path explains this surprising lapse.

Exhorting his children always to follow as their guide the teachings of the New Testament, a copy of which was packed with each son's personal effects on leaving home, Dickens wrote for their exclusive study and meditation a *Life of Our Lord,* prefacing it: "My Dear Children, I am very anxious that you should know something about the History of Jesus Christ. For everybody ought to know about Him. No one ever lived, who was so good, so kind, so gentle, and so sorry for all people who did wrong, or were in any way ill, or miserable, as he was. And as he is now in Heaven, where we hope to go, and all to meet each other after we are dead, and there to be happy always together, you never can think what a good place Heaven is, without knowing who he was and what he did."

* * *

How successful was Dickens as a father? For all his solicitous care, his close supervision of his children's education and religious training, his devoted love; for all his insistence on mutual trust and understanding, he was to be deeply disappointed.

Though he was well ahead of his time in making himself available to his children, in offering them sympathetic understanding, in planning their careers on the basis of their aptitudes, only one of his sons, Harry, lived up to expectations.

For Charley, his firstborn, the future at first looked promising because he seemed to be doing well at Eton. But, according to his father, he wanted "a habit of perseverance," having inherited from his mother "an indescribable lassitude of character."[28] When, after some uncertainties about his future, he decided on a mercantile career, he had all the necessary backing from his father. After several unsuccessful ventures, however, the last ending in bankruptcy and an indebtedness of a thousand pounds, Dickens finally made a place for him on his weekly journal, *All the Year Round.* After Dickens's death the journal continued for twenty-three years under Charley's editorship and was produced by the printing firm of which he and Evans, his brother-in-law, were partners. In addition Charley published some successful guide books on London, Paris, and the University of Cambridge; brought out some new editions, with introductions, of his father's works *(Pickwick Papers, Nicholas Nickleby, Dombey and Son, Reprinted Pieces, The Lazy Tour of Two Idle Apprentices, The Uncommercial Traveller);* and translated Schiller's *Der Neffe als Onkel.* On a tour of America (1888) he lectured on his father and read selections from his novels. The support of his large family (seven daughters and one son) compelled him to undertake any venture that might bolster his uncertain finances. Even so, he was not always prudent in his investments, as when he bought Gad's Hill, his father's last home, for nearly seven thousand pounds, an inflated price at the time because of its prestige. After his death in 1897 Queen Victoria granted his hard-pressed widow an annual pension of a hundred pounds.

The next child, Mamie, whom Henry James described as the "image of her father,"[29] displayed an abnormal coolness toward any suitable lover. At first indifferent to Percy Fitzgerald, one of Dickens's younger friends, she later ignored the attentions of an army officer, a William Lynch. Dickens is said to have admired him greatly and was disappointed by Mamie's attitude. Years later her brother Harry speculated on why his attractive sister had never married. "I think it was because she was so abso-

Fig. 8.   Charles Culliford Boz Dickens ("Flaster Floby")
(Dickens House)

Fig. 9.   Mary (Mamie) Dickens ("Mild Glo'ster")
(Dickens House)

lutely devoted to my father," he concluded.[30] One cannot help wondering whether he realized that this was actually a pathological devotion with the classic features of a father fixation. "My love for my father has never been touched by any other love," Mamie confessed in her published recollections. "I hold him in my heart of hearts as a man apart from all other beings."[31]

To Annie (Mrs. James T.) Fields of Boston she wrote an impassioned letter after her father's funeral, eulogizing him and declaring that it was "a glorious inheritance to have such blood flowing in one's veins." And, as if to dismiss any speculations about possible lovers, past or future, she affirmed her happiness at never having changed her name.[32]

Surviving Dickens by twenty-six years, Mamie grew increasingly restless. At first she lived with her maiden aunt, Georgina Hogarth. Then followed a succession of homes with friends, among them Sir William Humphrey, Bart., K. C. B., a Conservative member of Parliament, and his wife. Strong supporters of Muscular Christianity, the Humphreys initiated charitable projects from their home at Penton, near Andover, Hants. There in the severe winter of 1881 she joined them in arranging a Christmas celebration for some sixty children.[33] For a while she also lived with a clergyman and his wife, with whom she carried on philanthropic endeavors among the poor in Manchester.[34] In these efforts toward social betterment she must have been conscious of her father's influence. In her last years Mamie had lost the dainty charm of the Miss Dickens whom Henry James met in 1869, "ladylike in black silk and lace."[35] She had become a pathetic drifter with no settled abode, ill and lonely, seeking escape in alcohol.[36] Like her father she died at age fifty-eight, a coincidence she may have anticipated with morbid satisfaction during her last illness.

Katey, the third child, fared better, having both marriage and a successful career in art to give meaning to her life. Like her father in temperament, she was a great favorite with him, as her brothers and sister recognized. She was consequently the one they commissioned to beg special treats.[37] Less awed by her father, she spoke her mind with candor, an independence which he respected.

Ultimately the uncomfortable situation arising from her par-

Fig. 10.   Kate Macready Dickens ("Lucifer Box")
(Dickens House)

ents' domestic rupture in 1858 led Katey to marry a semi-invalid twelve years her senior, Charles Collins, Wilkie's younger brother. That his failing health caused Dickens uneasiness is evident from references in his letters. On the wedding day itself the father of the bride was under noticeable strain. After the guests had departed Mamie found him in Katey's empty room, his face buried in the folds of her wedding gown. "But for me," he sobbed, "Katey would not have left home."[38] Collins was to survive his father-in-law by only three years, after which Katey met and married Carlo Perugini, a rising young painter in her art circle. It was a happy marriage, enriched by a shared career.

It was with Katey that Dickens had his last heart-to-heart talk four days before his fatal seizure. Though she had come for counsel (she was thinking of going on the stage), the talk soon turned to other matters: Dickens's hopes for the unfinished *Edwin Drood,* and in particular, his personal life and the wish that he had been "a better father—a better man." To Gladys Storey, the confidante of her later years, Katey would speak leniently of her father's faults. "I know things about my father's character that no one else ever knew; he was not a good man, but he was not a fast man, but he was wonderful!"[39]

Though Katey did not blindly idolize her father, she may have understood him better than the others and have loved him even more—in that, unlike the doting Mamie, who worshiped an idol, Katey loved the whole human being, whose flaws she observed and admitted. From reticence and regard for family privacy she was unwilling to "give only half the truth about my father." She therefore burned the manuscript which she had prepared as a tribute to him.[40] But she arranged for a full revelation by her confidante after her death. As she lived to age eighty-nine, only Harry survived her. By 1939, when Gladys Storey's *Dickens and Daughter* was published, no member of the immediate family was living.

Not only in appraising her father's character, but also in assessing his literary genius, Katey came closer than his other children. This is borne out in her correspondence with George Bernard Shaw while the disposition of Dickens's letters to his wife was under consideration.[41] Not that she denied the validity of her father's exalted position. She allowed no comparison between "my father and any other artist in the world—. I believe my father to have been a man apart—as high above his fellow men—as the children of such great and exceptional men, are generally . . . below them."

Nonetheless, she made no attempt to condone her father's artistic shortcomings, as in the interpolated tales in *Pickwick Papers* and other books. Countering Shaw's suggestion that future critics might attribute these interpolations to another author, "an abysmally inferior hand," she maintained that "all the bad in my father's work is as entirely his own as the good." He would not have tolerated others working for him, she insisted. Passages which he wrote uncritically "in moments of fatigue or in what people call 'uninspired moments' he let pass as worthy to be placed with his best." Had they been the work of any other writer, he "would have put his veto on them." With probing insight she declared, "He could not have been the man he was without this weakness in his writing, as in his character. They explain the man." Obviously her intense attachment to her father could not distort her judgment. "My father was—as the girl in 'Caste' used to say 'a very clever man' but like all clever people he wrote and talked nonsense at times. *But that nonsense was his own.*" Like many a serious future critic, she deplored the popular image of Dickens held by the general reader. "If you could make the public understand," she pleaded, "that my father was not a joyous jocose gentleman walking with a plum pudding and a bowl of punch you would greatly oblige me."

For Walter, less individual than Katey, and not "so clever as Charley," Dickens held no academic ambitions. A "steady, amiable boy of good reliable capacity,"[42] he was to be prepared for a military career in India. He left England in July 1857 during the Indian Mutiny. A lieutenant in the twenty-sixth Native Infantry, he died suddenly of hematemesis (vomiting of blood) on 31 December 1863, shortly after he was to have been sent home on sick leave. Letters from his superior officer ultimately brought the sad account of accumulated unpaid debts. Temporarily halting his work on the tenth number of *Our Mutual Friend,* Dickens had to settle the "regimental part of poor Walter's wretched affairs—utterly incomprehensible, as they have always been," he complained.[43]

Fig. 11.   Walter Landor Dickens ("Young Skull")
(Dickens House)

The next son, Francis Jeffrey (Frank), also sent to India, lacked steadiness and purpose, so his father felt. Suffering from a painful stammer and occasional deafness, Frank, after spending some time in Germany to learn the language, had, because of his speech impediment, given up his ambition to become a doctor. A brief period on the staff of *All the Year Round* having shown him to be of little value there, he was nominated in 1863 to the Bengal Mounted Police. During his seven years in India he proved himself an excellent officer, but decided to return to England after his father's death. Fortunately, Dickens was spared the pain of seeing him lose his inheritance through speculation and wasteful spending. Through the efforts of his Aunt Georgina and his sisters he was offered a commission in the Canadian Northwest Mounted Police. Shortly after retiring he died suddenly in 1886 during a visit to Moline, Illinois.

The pattern of squandering money and accumulating debts, especially painful to Dickens because of his experience with his feckless father and several brothers, was to continue with the next son, Alfred Tennyson. Although the boy had spent six years preparing himself for a cadetship in artillery or engineering, he abandoned his plans for a military career. At one time he considered the tea business in Ceylon or China. Finally, after two years in London, he sailed for Australia in May 1865 to take up sheep farming, leaving behind many unpaid accounts with various haberdashers. Dickens had the embarrassment of settling a succession of bills for coats, trousers, silk scarves, French kid gloves, shirt studs and sleeve links, silk umbrellas, and bottles of scent.[44] When he left Australia years later, Alfred capitalized on his father's reputation by lecturing about him in England and America, his performances combining personal reminiscences and dramatic readings from the novels. Having become addicted to drink like his sister Mamie, he was not received at the home of his younger brother Harry while in London.[45] While on tour in New York he died in his hotel room on 2 January 1912 and was buried in the cemetery of Trinity Parish at 155th and Broadway.

Again the specter of extravagance haunted Dickens's household after the next son, Sydney Smith Haldimand, affectionately called "The Admiral," went to sea. So small that he "could easily have stowed himself and his wife and family of his own propor-

Fig. 12.   (left) Francis Jeffrey ("Chickenstalker") and (right) Henry
Fielding ("The Jolly Postboy") Dickens
(Dickens House)

Fig. 13. Alfred Tennyson Dickens ("Skittles") (at the time of his reading tour)
(Dickens House)

Fig. 14.   Sydney Smith Haldimand Dickens ("The Admiral")
(Dickens House)

tions" in his sea chest, wrote Dickens, he was a great favorite at home and on shipboard. While still a toddler Sydney had once roused his father to transports of admiration for "a wonderful piece of character, showing great readiness and resource." The child had run away, then returned to find the gate locked. "Open the gate!" he shouted, at the same time sending an enormous stone flying into the garden.[46] But once on his own he succumbed to the temptation of living beyond his means. Threatened with naval disciplinary action when he could not redeem his bills, he sought help from his father. "You can't understand how ashamed I am to appeal to you again," he wrote. Confessing to the real cause of his financial woes, an "insufficient strength of mind" to shake the habit of drinking with riotous companions, he pleaded, "If any promise for future amends can be relied on you have mine most cordially, but for God's sake assist me now." The result of refusal, he warned, would be "utter ruination."[47] But Sydney's promises were not to be trusted. Finally, convinced that removing one financial crisis simply cleared the way for another, Dickens gave up hope. His last letter to Sydney informed him that the doors of Gad's Hill would henceforth be shut to him. Nothing could have been more painful than abandoning this son, the deeply loved "Ocean Spectre," who had looked out so intently over the sea in childhood, the "Little Admiral," who had come home from training, "all eyes and gold buttons."

Toward his "last little child" Edward (Plorn), Dickens seemed to express affection more openly than with the others. Trotting beside his father on country walks, the little fellow roused tender amusement by his childish prattle. The perfection of his baby body caused his father to boast that the child was "in wonderful condition, perpetually running about on two mottled legs, and falling down on jagged stones that never seem to hurt [him]." On an early birthday, in bed with measles, Plorn was portrayed in whimsical and rich detail: "[He] goes to sleep among a large cart of real timber drawn by two grey horses; a Noah's Ark with all the animals out walking, in company with Noah, Ham, Shem and Japhet, Mrs. N., Mrs. H., Mrs. S., and Mrs. J.; the Camp at Chobham and four brass cannon; a farm-yard; a box of bricks; a clown in a washing-tub, driving two geese; four crusts of buttered toast;

Fig. 15.   Edward Bulwer Lytton Dickens ("Plornishmaroontigoonter")
(Dickens House)

all the cannon-balls (which roll into bed and tickle him); and I don't know what besides."[48]

But all his father's love could not ward off the lassitude and instability that had plagued nearly all of Plorn's brothers. His general inaptitude for learning and his poor record at school persuaded Dickens to prepare him for sheep farming in Australia. Accordingly, after some training to acquaint him with life in the bush, he was sent to Melbourne in September 1868 to join his brother Alfred. It was the hardest parting of all. "He seemed to me to become once more my youngest and favourite child. . . ," Dickens wrote after seeing him off, "and I did not think I could have been so shaken."[49] Dickens's death in 1870 mercifully spared him the pain of watching this favorite son become involved in heavy gambling losses, followed by appeals to Harry for loans that were never paid off or even acknowledged.

Only one son, Harry, the second youngest, did not disappoint his father. Of him Katey wrote in one of her letters to Shaw: "Out of our large family of nine children, there was only *one* who ever seemed to me really quite sane."[50] Already demonstrating admirable steadiness and dedicated industry while still in grammar school, he appeared to be the one who could benefit from a university education. His dependability, however, did not exempt him from close supervision. Once he was settled in Cambridge, his father wrote him a frank, businesslike letter detailing financial matters. "We must have no shadow of debt," Dickens warned. An annual allowance of £250, which he called "handsome," should take care of Harry's needs, especially since his wines were supplied from the family's stock at Gad's Hill. Reminded that his father had never had any outside help since childhood and had always worked hard for his money, Harry was told once again what his brothers had heard *ad nauseam:* "You know that you are one of many heavy charges on me." This charge, he was given to understand, could be diminished by improving the advantages of his "past expensive education."[51]

Harry took the admonition to heart. Passing his "little go" at Trinity Hall with honors, he went on to win Trinity's best mathematical scholarship, which carried an annual stipend of £50. Breaking the news of his latest success while he and his father were out walking, Harry felt hurt when the response was only a terse

"Capital! Capital!" Suddenly, halfway up the road, Dickens clasped Harry's hand and exclaimed, "God bless you, my boy!"[52] Such reticence was typical, a "habit of suppression," as Dickens himself diagnosed it, "which now belongs to me, which I know is no part of my original nature, but which makes me chary of showing my affections, even to my children, except when they are very young."[53] Years later Harry was to describe his father's reserve as "an intense dislike of letting himself go in private life." Although his children knew "he was devotedly attached to them, there was still a kind of reserve . . . which seemed to occasionally come as a cloud between us and which I never quite understood."[54] However gratified by Harry's honors, his father still had some reservations about his promise, especially after being repeatedly disappointed in his other sons. "I hope he will get a fellowship at last," he told Macready, "but I have learned to moderate my transports as to hopeful children."[55] What a pity he did not live to see his son honored as an eminent barrister and judge—Sir Henry Fielding Dickens!

Why was Dickens to be disappointed in all but one of his sons? Surely no man ever took his paternal responsibilities more seriously. "I hope you will always be able to say in after life, that you had a kind father," he wrote in a farewell letter to Plorn.[56] How had this kindness miscarried? Having played with his children when they were small, recorded their antics, and carefully planned their education, he had unquestionably been a concerned parent. Certainly no father had ever been closer to his sons and daughters in their early years. Indeed, in his love of excitement and surprise, his exuberant delight in their amusements, his sympathetic understanding of their trivial vexations, he had enjoyed unusual empathy with them. It was as if, deprived of his own boyhood after leaving Chatham, he was desperately intent on recapturing his lost years through them. In him the child and the parent were coexistent. It must be remembered, however, that he experienced his happiest relations with his children in their early years, but seemingly never grew up with them. Actually, he dreaded the prospect of growing old, and thus preferred to be addressed as "Venerables" instead of "Grandfather" when his grandchildren came along. "Childhood is usually so beautiful and engaging," he observed in "Where We

Stopped Growing" (*HW*, 1 January 1853), "that ... there is a mournful shadow of the common lot in the notion of its changing and fading into anything else."

As "a child of larger growth" among his children, however, Dickens may have dominated their work and play too much. His taking over the building of Charley's toy theatre has already been cited as an example. Such close supervision and domination also applied to the Twelfth Night festivities. "I found the children getting up a dull charade," Dickens reported while preparations for Charley's birthday were already in progress.[57] Unwilling to see his children in an uninspired performance of their own devising, he promptly masterminded an elaborate production of *Tom Thumb*, complete with an assisting cast of adults from his own troupe. In denying the small actors the pleasure of initiating their own projects, he prevented them from exercising their imagination and ingenuity. Such a course inevitably saps initiative. Though in modern terms Dickens must be commended for making himself available to his children, a wise parent "watches the drama of growth, but resists the desire to intervene too often."[58]

Equally unwise was Dickens's obsession with tidiness. The daily inspections of rooms, the insistence that hats and coats be kept on assigned pegs, the examination of garments for fresh stains, and the regimented routine of the household irritated the boys. However valuable their early training in orderliness, forceful imposition may have had a negative effect. It could even explain Frank's stammer, for such a speech impediment is often a symptom of underlying nervous maladjustment.[59] It may also have had some bearing on his boyhood sleep walking.

That Dickens's sons sometimes regarded their father as a martinet is attested by Harry's reminiscences. Though they dared not express their displeasure openly, "our resentment," he says, "took the more insidious form of deeply whispered mutterings among ourselves on the subject of 'slavery,' 'degradation,' and so forth, which, while being somewhat transpontine in their character and wholly ineffective in their results, still served as a kind of safety valve and helped to soothe our ruffled feelings."[60]

In addition to orderliness Dickens demanded peace and quiet. Under strain when he was meeting monthly deadlines, not to mention other commitments, he could not always conceal his annoyance at the least disturbance. Completely absorbed in his work and so tense that even the dropping of a spoon would pain him, he was irritated by the very presence of his sons in the home. To Wilkie Collins he complained of their noise, especially of Walter, then fourteen and the loudest: "Why a boy of that age should seem to have on at all times, 150 pairs of double-soled boots, I don't know."[61] As late as 1863 he was still disturbed by unusual activity. "This place is at present pervaded by boys to a fearful extent," he again complained to Collins. "They boil over (if an affectionate parent may mention it) all over the house."[62]

Added to his complaints of even routine noise was his constant harping on thrift. Too frequently reminded that their father had worked hard for his money and that they were a heavy drain on him, all but one of his sons built up a subconscious resistance to his advice by overspending their allowance and ignoring their debts. After all, did not their father maintain his home on a rather lavish scale with its rich and showy furnishings and elaborate dinner parties? As for his wardrobe, was it not costly, extensive, and flamboyant? Brought up in this environment, the boys naturally assumed that they were entitled to expenditures in keeping with the opulence of their home. They learned to shrug off Dickens's constant reminders that he found their personal expenses a burden. "I can't get my hat on in consequence of the extent to which my hair stands on end at the costs and charges of these boys," he exclaimed in 1868 to Dolby, his reading manager. "Why was I ever a father!"[63]

Interspersed with such complaints were flippant references to the size of his family. Though, as already stated, he found babies irresistible, announcing each new arrival as "a chopping boy," a "brilliant boy of unheard-of-dimensions," he became progressively less exuberant until he declared after the last, "I am not quite clear that I particularly wanted the latter." Facetiously he wrote to Mrs. Gore of a plan to intercede with the "Bishop of London to have a little service in Saint Paul's beseeching that I may be considered to have done enough towards my country's population." And he promised not to give her a godchild.[64] One wonders whether his children were aware of his mocking attitude, either through overhearing such remarks or listening to some of his tasteless jokes. According to one source he was not above crudely calling attention, with pointed allusions, to the condition of a pregnant woman, embarrassing all who heard him, including the "subject of his obstetric wit."[65]

As his sons grew older, Dickens let them sense his disappointment in them. Preferring to believe that their instability was inherited from their mother, he confided his pessimism to his friends. To W. H. Willis, his subeditor, he complained that his boys had a "curse of limpness on them" and an "inadaptability to anything."[66] To Wilkie Collins he wrote ruefully: "I am so undoubtedly one of the sons of Toil—and fathers of children— that I expect to be presently presented with a smock frock, a pair of leather breeches, and a pewter watch, for having brought up the largest family ever known with the smallest disposition to do anything for themselves."[67] When Charles Albert Fechter, the Alsatian actor, told Longfellow that all Dickens's success went for nothing because he was unhappy in his family, Mrs. James T. Fields, who overheard the remark, could not help wondering "how much too much of this the children have had to hear."[68] Whatever they did hear, or merely sensed, would certainly not have inspired them to succeed.

There is, moreover, a question about the children's capacity for achievement. Katey, for one, had no illusions about the shortcomings of her brothers and sister. "I think," she told Shaw, "the children of a very clever man who uses his brain all day long— have a very poor chance of having much themselves—and seldom if ever resemble their father in any one particular." Except for Harry, she explained, each of the Dickens children, though sane, had "a crack somewhere."[69] (Harry, apparently, had inherited his father's steadiness, determination, and industry. Though less gifted, in later years he often reminded his Aunt Georgina of Dickens, especially when on special occasions he gave public readings from the novels.) It has been speculated that, the creative energy of a great author having spent itself in his imaginative work, a lesser vigor is transmitted to his offspring through weakened sperm. Whatever the merits of this theory, there can be no quarrel with John Stuart Mill's thesis that "the children of energetic parents frequently grow up unenergetic, because they lean on their parents, and the parents are energetic for them"

(*Autobiography*, Chap. 1). Convinced that they could never measure up to the demands of genius, Dickens's sons seem to have viewed their mediocrity as inevitable. As Plorn was to remark in later years, "Sons of great men are not usually as great as their fathers. You cannot get two Charles Dickens in one generation."[70]

Determined to counteract in his children any early indications of the pecuniary recklessness that had ruined his father and several brothers, Dickens wanted to make his sons self-sufficient against the time when they could no longer fall back on him for support. All but dependable Harry were therefore sent from home early to find their special "groove": Sydney, at thirteen; Charley, Walter, and Edward, at sixteen; Frank, at nineteen; Alfred, at twenty. Even as he prepared them for their ventures, Dickens continued to complain about mounting expenses. Early discouraging reports evoked renewed laments over his sons' "lassitude, their want of perseverance, their inability to follow a fixed purpose."

Did it ever occur to Dickens that his sons' instability might have had some connection with what he himself called the "skeleton in the domestic closet," the deepening rift between himself and his wife, which brought on his dark moods and his restlessness? According to him, the incompatibility had developed gradually, beginning soon after the birth of the second child in 1838 and becoming unbearable in the 1850s. If one may believe his statements, his wife's occasional jealousy of various women, compounded by neurotic outbursts, had widened the rift until domestic tranquility could never be restored. Having borne ten children (one died in infancy) in fifteen years, not to mention several miscarriages, Catherine Dickens had been unable to keep pace with her energetic husband. As the Newcastle *Chronicle* would characterize her some years later (9 March 1889), she was "seemingly quite without natural power, or spirit, or natural force of manner to guide or control such a volatile character as that of Charles Dickens." Her physical clumsiness and bulging plumpness, worsened by constant childbearing, had often made her the butt of his tart jokes. Intellectually, moreover, she had been forced by repeated confinement to restrict her interests and social contacts, so that she had fallen behind her husband in mental breadth. With his friends and their scintillating repartee she must have felt out of place.

How much of this domestic unhappiness erupted in the open is, of course, a matter of speculation. But there can be little doubt that some of it filtered through to the children. Close observers of their parents, children, according to one authority, react emotionally to the home situation. If all is well, they feel secure and do not waste psychic energy in worry. But where they sense parental friction they "feel anxious and guilty—anxious because their home is threatened, guilty because of their actual or imagined role in the family friction. Justifiably or not, children assume that they are the cause of the domestic strife."[71] Such anxiety may well have been one cause of Frank's stammer, which began in the 1850s when his parents' discord was building and his father was unusually tense and irritable, waiting for "the skeleton in my domestic closet" to break forth.[72]

Once domestic tranquility had been irrevocably shattered, the Dickenses finally agreed to a legal separation. According to the terms of the contract, completed in April 1852, Catherine was to live away from the family in a London home provided by her husband. All the children but the oldest, Charley, remained with their father. Though they were free to visit their mother, they seldom did so for fear of displeasing him. This neglect must have made them feel guilty, especially the daughters, who were always in London for the social season. The time they might have devoted to their mother was spent in activities which won them the censure of Mrs. Grundy. One of their father's friends, John Frederick Lehmann, scolded that "those two girls are going to the devil as fast as can be. . . . I hear . . . society is beginning to fight shy of them." Mamie, he predicted, might "blaze up in fireworks any day." And Katey, married without love to the ailing Charles Collins, was "burning away both character and . . . health slowly but steadily."[73]

One would welcome details. Had the girls gone about unchaperoned? (After all, Katey, as a married woman, was technically qualified to chaperone her sister.) Had they frequented restaurants—taboo for ladies in society? Had they appeared at balls in too daring décolletage? Whatever the gossip, it must have been neither widespread nor long-lived, for it did not prevent Mamie from being presented at Queen Victoria's rigid court less than a decade later.

Coming at a time when the five youngest sons, ranging in age from six to thirteen, still needed the security of a normal home life, the domestic rupture set the family apart from other households. To be sure, Catherine's younger sister, Georgina Hogarth, was still in charge. Having been with the Dickenses from the age of fourteen, she had gradually made herself indispensable by taking over the early instruction of the children and the management of domestic matters. According to Dickens her nieces and nephews felt more comfortable with her than with their own mother. But when she refused to leave with her sister after the legal separation, both her family and respectable society were outraged. As she accordingly became the subject of unsavory and malicious gossip, Dickens bristled with indignation. Reverberations from the fury he unleashed against the scandalmongers and reports of his demand for public apologies may well have reached his children.

Also damaging would have been their suspicions concerning the Gad's Hill visits of Ellen Ternan, the young actress now generally believed to have been Dickens's mistress. Prevented on legal grounds from obtaining a divorce and marrying her, he settled for unrestricted access to the house he leased for her in London. The older children must have realized that this youthful beauty was more than just a good friend of the family. But perhaps, like their Aunt Georgina, they condoned their father's conduct by affirming that "a man of genius ought not to be judged with the common herd of men."[74] Such a rationale could not insulate them, however, against the gossip that they must have overheard in their social circle. "There is hardly one actress in London at all young and handsome who was not scandalized by having her name associated with this affair," declared an anonymous reporter in the Newscastle *Chronicle* (4 June 1858). "But the most generally accepted version pointed to a young and clever actress in the Haymarket company, and it would not be fair to give her name in connection with what is now an exploded scandal. So far did it proceed, however, that it is said Mrs. Dickens herself wrote a letter to a member of the company stating that, though it was true she and her husband had some differences, yet she felt it her due to the lady, whose name was so freely implicated, to say that she was not the cause of them." (Such a letter would likely have been written at Dickens's insistence, may even have been dictated by him.)

Because Dickens appeared in public with Ellen Ternan while traveling between England and France, his conduct continued to provoke censure. Typical, perhaps, was the indignant reaction of a fellow passenger on the Boulogne Packet. Having seen Dickens with a "lady not his wife, nor his sister-in-law," she deplored his bad taste in parading "the unwarrantable acts of his private life so as to give public scandal." She charged, further, that he lacked "the instincts of a gentleman," for he "strutted about the deck with the air of a man bristling with self-importance!" It was her conviction that "no one can afford to overlook his immoral life."[75]

Whatever the sources and the nature of the strictures directed against their father, the children must have found them disturbing. As for the younger sons, such glimmerings of the truth as they may have surmised, together with an uneasiness over their mother's abnormal isolation, would hardly have helped them to "follow a fixed purpose."

Dickens's fatherhood, then, although characterized by deep affection and concern, brought its toll in heartaches. Some of these may be attributed to his overzealousness in seeking to spare his children the insecurity of his own boyhood. Still others may have resulted from his absorption in the world of his imagination, where the children of his "fancy," his dream children, were often closer to him than his real children with all their failings. In short, he may have been unable to bridge the gap between idealized and flawed children. Finally, there were the disturbing events leading to the domestic rupture, as well as the separation itself. All these left an imprint on the sons in their formative years. So, although Dickens had only the best intentions for his family and was well ahead of his time in demanding that children be granted their rights as individuals, repeated disappointments may have led him to secret doubts of his adequacy as a father. Perhaps his daughter Katey was right when she told G. B. Shaw, "Men of genius . . . ought not to be allowed to have children."[76] In this belief, moreover, Dickens had already anticipated her when he exclaimed jestingly, in words that could be interpreted on several levels, "Why was I ever a father!"

Chapter 4
"Into the Care-Laden World"

"Through this little gate, she passed out of childhood into the care-laden world."

Little Dorrit (I, 7)

Repeatedly frustrated as he prepared his sons to move "out of childhood into the care-laden world," Dickens, as previously stated, confided his bitter disappointment to his close friends. His frank comments have led his critics to accuse him of being kinder to his fictional creations than to the "living members of his hearth" ("as conspicuously fair to the children of his imagination as he was unfair to those of the flesh").[1] Some have gone so far as to condemn Georgina Hogarth for the sons' early separation from home and friends, arguing that she wanted Dickens and Gad's Hill to herself. Nothing could be further from the truth. To ensure a smoothly functioning household after the domestic rupture, Miss Hogarth refused to consider marriage and a home of her own, ignoring public censure by remaining at Gad's Hill as Dickens's housekeeper and joint hostess with Mamie. As the counselor and loving companion of the younger sons, she helped to minimize the damage arising from their mother's absence. Later, as they grew up and left home, it was she who regularly corresponded with them, encouraging them as they faced some difficult adjustment, rejoicing when they occasionally reported a successful venture, and constantly reminding them of their father's deep affection. After all, had she wished to be sole mistress of Gad's Hill, she could have maneuvered to have Mamie banished. But between aunt and niece there was never the slightest hint of rivalry. "When I speak of my

64

Aunt," Mamie declared in later years, "it is of Georgina Hogarth, *the* Aunt *par excellence*, the beloved and faithful Friend, who has been, as long as I can remember her, always the same, true, reliable loving companion and counselor."[2]

So it was not a scheming Georgina Hogarth who sent the nephews "into the care-laden world," nor was it their father's ruthless disregard of the pain which such an early separation must have inflicted upon boys of tender age. It went deeper than that. Always at the back of his mind Dickens harbored the nagging fear that his sons would turn out to be like his father, who constantly needed to be rescued from financial crises. For years John Dickens had been a heavy drain on him, having again been arrested for debt in 1834, still accumulating bills that were never paid, and even asking the publishers for advances on his son's next novel. For immediate cash he even sold autographs and sheets of manuscript. "How long he is, growing up to be a m[an]!" Dickens complained.[3] On a previous occasion he had, not surprisingly, reacted calmly to his father's temporary disappearance: "I own that his absence from home does not give me great earnestness, knowing how he is apt to get out of the way when anything goes wrong."[4] Though Dickens could regard his father with mingled amusement and affection, immortalizing his florid style in *David Copperfield*, he was less indulgent later in *Little Dorrit*. There a begging letter from the parasitic William Dorrit to Arthur Clennam has an unmistakable echo of John Dickens, with its pretense of "having been disappointed of a remittance" from the City and its assumed reluctance at having been forced to "take up his pen" to entreat the recipient to "advance him Three Pounds Ten Shillings upon his I. O. U. which he begged to enclose" (I, 22). When, in an effort to remove his father from further entanglements in London, Dickens in June 1839 settled his parents at Mile End Cottage near Exeter, they felt abused and sent him "hateful, sneering letters."[5] In July, after a complaining note from his mother, Dickens exploded to his close friend John Forster: "I do swear that I am sick at heart with both her and father too, and think that this *is* too much."[6] For years John Dickens's peccadillos were to involve his son in painful embarrassments. Time and again Charles had to pay the old man's debts, hopelessly declaring on one occasion to Thomas Mitton, his legal adviser, "He is certain to do it again." His parents, as well as other dependents, looked upon him "as something to be plucked and torn to pieces for their advantage." And he added bitterly, "My soul sickens at the thought of them."[7] In desperation he again confided to Thomas Mitton some months later, "For anything like the damnable Shadow which this father of mine casts upon my face, there never was—except in a nightmare."[8] (Once the father's offenses had died with him in 1851, the son reverted to his early affection, remarking to Forster that "I regard [him] as a better man, the longer I live."[9])

Just as prone as their father to mismanage their affairs were three of Dickens's brothers. Frederick, never able to get along on his income, applied repeatedly for help until he finally had to be refused. Alfred, the oldest, died penniless, leaving a widow and five children to be provided for. Augustus, the youngest, deserted a blind wife and ran off to America, where he sent back appeals to Dickens for help. On his death he left a mistress and three small children destitute in Chicago.[10]

Having had more than his share of "poor relations" to deal with, Dickens took steps he considered necessary to prevent his sons from repeating the family pattern. When, however, unsatisfactory reports confirmed his fears that they had inherited their grandfather's and uncles' weaknesses, as well as their mother's "lassitude," he could retreat into the realm of creative imagination. There his dream children, unlike his real family, unfolded according to his own design. They became a compelling presence among whom their creator was oblivious to any other company. His son Charley tells of walking with him at Gad's Hill on various occasions, completely ignored as his father strode at his usual four-mile-an-hour pace, eyes straight ahead, lips working in the throes of creation. Once delivered of an idea, he would drop back into the real world and resume conversation as if there had been no break. Such behavior Charley would observe again on their last walk together: "Although his eyes were bent upon me and he seemed to be looking earnestly, he did not see me. . . . He was, in fact, unconscious for the moment of my existence. He was in dreamland with *Edwin Drood*."[11]

It should be emphasized that with one exception Dickens's dream children had no genesis in the world of reality. Though they might share incidental mannerisms with youngsters in general, none can be said to resemble his own sons and daughters. For only one fictional child, the most dominant of all, did Dickens take his model from a real child—that twelve-year-old boy, that "little hind" who had been thrust down the social ladder into the humiliating hell of Warren's Blacking Warehouse. In his crusade to improve the lot of children everywhere Dickens drew upon his early experiences, realizing that they resembled those endured by countless children in industrial England, that the opportunity denied him had also been denied them, that the loneliness induced by his parents' neglect had also oppressed hundreds who drifted aimlessly about London, little nomads who slept in doorways and arcades or found shelter with criminals and prostitutes. Once his bitter memories had fused with what he saw as the general condition of his century, he imposed on his dream children an idealized image of childhood. With his view that the young have a pre-Adamic endowment of goodness which is constantly attacked by the evils about them, he looked upon life as a struggle between the spiritual values symbolized by the child and the blind worship of monetary gain pervading society, a struggle between inherent honesty and rapacity. Like Carlyle in *Past and Present* he asked the probing question: "To whom, then, is this wealth of England wealth? Who is it that it blesses; makes happier, wiser, beautifuler, in any way better?" (I, i). Like Carlyle, moreover, he found nothing to reassure him as he considered the fate of his country: "We have departed far away from the *Laws* of this Universe, and behold now lawless Chaos and inane Chimera is ready to devour us!" (I, 5).

As Dickens made his boyhood insecurity the pivot of his mature art, he was actually joining a growing movement to protest society's callous treatment of the young. In 1830 Bulwer-Lytton had already published *Paul Clifford*, whose plot involves the fate of a boy sentenced to death by a judge who turns out to be his own father. Another early novel of social protest, Frances Trollope's *Michael Armstrong, the Factory Boy* (1840), portrays the abuses inflicted upon an orphan indentured to a cruel mill owner. And in 1841 Charlotte Elizabeth [Browne Tonna] recounted the painful adventures of another orphan in *Helen Fleetwood*, whose heroine goes to work at the age of sixteen in a textile mill, loses her health because of the long hours and intolerable conditions, and is finally released by a merciful death. No doubt Dickens knew these and other early examples of social protest. Convinced that the time was right for novelists to awaken the public conscience, he used his fiction to analyze his own boyhood experiences and to control the emotions they evoked. In the process he came to see delinquent parents as the microcosm of a sick state that had failed its constituents. If the state was to be saved, he concluded, a start must be made in the home. Accordingly he began to focus on parent-child relationships. The inadequate parents of his fiction would parallel the incompetent governors responsible for England's social and civil malaise.

Various influences may have steered Dickens to this emphasis. One was his daily contact with the poor children whom he saw in the streets. Some of his intimate impressions he gained firsthand from the Ragged Schools and the housing projects he had helped Angela Burdett-Coutts to organize. His letters to her show his concern for the children's well-being, their religious instruction, and their preparation for future usefulness. Where their parents and the state had failed them, Miss Coutts's charitable endeavors provided the necessary guidance and support.

Another influence, Dickens's dependence on the New Testament for moral guidance, cannot be overemphasized, especially the glorification of childish innocence. "Suffer the little children to come unto me, and forbid them not; for to such belongeth the kingdom of God," Christ had admonished His disciples (Luke 18:16). For Dickens such admonition would demand the sternest measures in dealing with child neglect and abuse. He was ever mindful how Christ, taking a child in His arms, had declared that "Whosoever shall receive such little children in my name, receiveth me" (Mark 9:37). And he endorsed emphatically the New Testament injunction against anyone who should "offend one of these little ones."

Unquestionably the most important single event that returned Dickens to his own boyhood, reinforcing his concern for the lonely and neglected child and having special impact on his later novels, was the death of John Dickens on 31 March 1851. This loss, together with the approach of middle age, brought back the past, the humiliation at Warren's Blacking Warehouse, the lonely evenings in the London streets, the hunger after a week's wages had been spent. His father's death, then, simply sustained his crusade for the violated child, a mission already successfully initiated by his earlier novels. In his later work his handling of social implications became more probing, more devastatingly satirical.

The more Dickens relived his past, the sharper grew his focus on the interrelations of social and personal disorders. Hence his novels present few normal family situations. Parents seldom maintain a healthy relationship with their children, most of whom, consequently, experience a troubled youth. Many others are orphans.

"The Great Father who requires that His children should love Him, requires also that they should love their earthly parents," Dickens wrote in a letter of condolence to George Beadnell.[12] Finding this love absent in many of the homes he had observed, he took up the cause of the lonely and alienated child in need of identity. Into the fabric of his narrative he wove the recurring patterns of parent-child relationships that became pivotol to his work. Four of these patterns are so persistent as to merit detailed examination in the second half of this study: they center on (1) orphans who are left to the mercy of surrogate parents, (2) unwanted or slighted children who must cope with hard or insensitive parents, (3) misguided or corrupted children who are the products of pernicious parental influence, and (4) exploited children who must assume the responsibilities of indifferent or ineffectual parents. To be sure, these categories do not cover all the situations involving parent-child relationships in Dickens's novels. Still, so frequently do these patterns appear that they serve as a unifying design.

Although Dickens's own fatherhood was fraught with disappointment and sorrow, the children of his "fancy" would not fail him. These creations, inspired by early experience and later observation, became the basis of his studies of society. The orphans, the abandoned nomads, the inherently innocent but misguided juveniles, the victims of adult apathy and cruelty—all fired Dickens's indignation over the inhumanity of a state that would tolerate the destruction of its very foundation. To counter the social callousness of the age, Dickens peopled his pages with children who would arouse the public conscience. Like the world of fiction, which begins with observable elements of everyday existence, only to be metamorphosed into a place seen solely through the eyes of the novelist, so the children, however realistic at first glance, are idealized creations and come to life only when seen against the background of the Dickens world. Unlike too many actual Victorian street children, irreversibly corrupted by their environment, they retain their inherent goodness and conquer the evil forces pitted against them. Some assume responsibilities far beyond their years; others mature by facing every challenge. As "a fond parent to every child of my fancy," Dickens used these dream children to promote a society where the young and innocent would not be forced to emerge prematurely through the gate of childhood "into the care-laden world." With this mission to spur his art, he attained his zenith.

Part Two

A Nation's Glory, or a Nation's Shame?

"If the State would begin its work and duty at the beginning, and would with the strong hand take ... children out of the streets, while they are yet children, and wisely train them, it would make them a part of England's glory, not its shame—of England's strength, not its weakness."

"The Short-Timers" *(The Uncommercial Traveller)*

Chapter 5

"The Lovingest Duty and Thanks of the Orphan"

"... will you give him [Mr. Peggotty] the lovingest duty and thanks of the orphan, as he was ever more than a father to?"

David Copperfield (Chap. 51)

With none of his dream children did Dickens identify more fully than with the orphans, who comprise the largest single group in his novels. There is hardly a major character who has not lost either a father or mother, or both. Cast adrift on his own during the Marshalsea period, Dickens had himself been virtually an orphan for a brief time. "I was so young and childish, and so little qualified—how could I be otherwise?—to undertake the whole charge of my existence," he was to reflect later in his Autobiographical Fragment.

With the scars of this neglected period never to fade, he would always view the world as peopled by orphans, the victims of society's indifference and abuse. It is not surprising, therefore, that he chose an orphan for his central character in *Oliver Twist*, one of his earliest works. With Oliver, the "parish child—the orphan of a workhouse—the humble half-starved drudge—to be cuffed and buffeted through the world—despised by all, and pitied by none" (Chap. 1), he intended, according to a statement originally included in his Preface, "to show ... the principle of Good surviving through every adverse circumstance and triumphing at last." Rebuked by the workhouse beadle as a "naughty orphan which nobody can't love" (Chap. 4), starved and beaten, Oliver holds his inherent goodness inviolate.

In emphasizing Oliver's inborn integrity, Dickens was clearly following the pre-Adamic tradition that had already found full expression in such Romantics as Blake and Wordsworth. And, as stated in the preceding chapter, the New Testament lends its support to childhood innocence. No one, Christ warned, could enter the kingdom of heaven without becoming as a little child (Matthew 18:2). But it was not until Rousseau proclaimed their natural piety that children were freed from the bonds of sectarian bias and the Puritan emphasis on original sin.

For Blake, who saw Christ in every child and who was himself childlike, expressing unconventional ideas in child language without reticence, the helplessness of youth beset by social wrongs held a strong appeal. For Wordsworth the child was endowed with a natural integrity and insight, being at one with its maker, "trailing clouds of glory . . . from God, who is our home." The child was the "best Philosopher," one who could read the "eternal deep." But inevitably environment taints native innocence and "shades of the prison house begin to close/ Upon the growing Boy."

Dickens, like Blake and Wordsworth, also realized that innocence is destroyed by sinister forces in society. In *Oliver Twist, Dombey and Son, Bleak House,* and elsewhere, Dickens parallels Blake's indictments of unloving parents and of such social institutions as the almshouse and the church. This is not to suggest that he consciously echoed, or even knew, such lyrics as "The Chimney-sweeper," "The Little Vagabond," "The Little Boy Lost," "London," and "Holy Thursday." Their essence permeated the air as the century advanced. "Holy Thursday" *(Songs of Experience)* especially, with its portrayal of organized charity—"Babes reduc'd to misery/ Fed with cold usurous hand"—calls up the inevitable comparison with *Oliver Twist.*

In this early novel the emphasis is still Manichaean, with the principle of good eventually triumphing over evil. In later novels, in which characters are irrevocably scarred by early environment (Estella, Louisa Gradgrind, Arthur Clennam), Dickens, in indicting those charged with the care of children, makes their abuses symptomatic of a disordered society.

Throughout his career Dickens depended upon irony as an effective weapon of assault. Through wild and humorous exaggeration, the whole system of nineteenth-century parish charity, with its corrupt officials and flagrant abuses, is held up to ridicule. *Oliver Twist* is a rich mine of such early examples. The gin-drinking matron of the workhouse is facetiously dubbed the "benevolent protectress" of the orphans. She is said to know "what was good for children; and she had a very accurate perception of what was good for herself," namely, appropriating "the greater part of the weekly stipend to her own use . . ." (Chap. 2). Another butt of Dickens's trenchant humor is Bumble, the parish beadle, referred to as the "farmer of infants." His description of the parish board which plans to apprentice Oliver to a master chimney sweep becomes preposterous when the members are called "the kind and blessed gentlemen which is so many parents to you, Oliver, when you have none of your own" (Chap. 3). But even Bumble, however callous he may be in dispersing orphans, cannot ignore Oliver's cry of desperation before being apprenticed to an undertaker: "So lonely, sir!" pleads the boy, "so very lonely! Everybody hates me." His grim business momentarily interrupted, "Mr. Bumble regarded Oliver's piteous and helpless look, with some astonishment, for a few seconds; hemmed three or four times in a husky manner; and, after muttering something about 'that troublesome cough,' bade Oliver dry his eyes and be a good boy" (Chap. 4). Dickens's use of childish innocence to move the hardest heart was to become a recurring device in his later work.

The board itself is an object of derision because of its absurd claims for the workhouse as public benefactor: "—the people liked it! It was a regular place of public entertainment for the poorer classes; a tavern where there was nothing to pay; a public breakfast, dinner, tea, and supper all the year round; a brick and mortar elysium, where it was all play and no work" (Chap. 2). Seventeen years later this mocking tone was to be echoed in *Hard Times*, where Gradgrind and Bounderby insist that the oppressed people of Coketown live "upon the best," that they buy fresh butter and require Mocha coffee, that they reject all "but the prime parts of meat" (I, 5).

After suffering the abuses and privations of the workhouse system, Oliver faces the severest tests of his innate honesty. A forbidding setting foreshadows the dark forces that threaten him. In one of London's worst slums, a place of narrow, muddy streets, he meets drunken men and women "wallowing in filth."

The air he breathes is "impregnated with filthy odours" (Chap. 8). In this wretched world of slime, the physical manifestation of spiritual depravity, Fagin, his toothless gums "disclosing such fangs as should have been a dog's or cat's," crawls forth at night in search of some rich offal. That he is meant to embody the devil himself is clear from the comments of his fellow criminals.[1] When the dog growls at Fagin, Bill Sikes shouts, "Lie down, you stupid brute! Don't you know the devil when he's got a great-coat on?" (Chap. 19). And Nancy, unable to free herself from Fagin's curse, calls him "devil" and "worse than devil to me" (Chap. 46). In this connection it may be noted that Dickens describes Fagin's "repulsive face . . . [as] obscured by a quantity of matted red hair," a feature commonly associated with the devil as portrayed in medieval plays.

Though not cast in the demonic mold, Monks is as menacing as Fagin, whom he has hired to destroy his half-brother, Oliver, by forcing him to follow a life of crime and thereby forfeit his inheritance. Monks is described as dark and haggard, eyes sunk deep in his head, lips often "discoloured with the marks of teeth," hands "covered with wounds of tooth marks." In him "all evil passions, vice, and profligacy" have "festered" until they have "found a vent in a hideous disease" (syphilis?) which has made his face "an index" of his mind (Chap. 49). On his throat is a broad "red mark, like a burn or scald," obviously intended to suggest the brand of Cain. For he has sworn to hound Oliver "to the very gallows-foot," even to have him murdered (Chap. 51).

Unlike Fagin, with his avarice and cunning, or Monks, with his venomous hatred, Sikes is only a typical nineteenth-century underworld character, rough, ill-tempered, brutal. Loud and menacing, he can even cow the wily Fagin, who depends on him to execute the more daring robberies. Eventually his uncontrollable temper, together with his brutality, destroys him and dooms Fagin's lair.

In that lair Oliver at first perceives Fagin as a kindly old man, fond of children. He responds with hearty laughter at the handkerchief-snatching game, not yet aware of its purpose. To the juvenile gang with whom Oliver shelters, Fagin serves *in loco parentis*. The boys have no home but his lair, a preparatory school which trains them for the gallows. Their schoolmaster, it must be

Fig. 16. Oliver Introduced to the Respectable Old Gentleman, illustration by George Cruikshank, from *Oliver Twist*

admitted, practices an advanced educational philosophy, one which includes certain of Dickens's own precepts of juvenile education. By spirited educational games, encouragement through praise, prowess with the toasting fork at midnight suppers, and always by example of his own criminal virtuosity, Fagin inspires such an urge toward learning, such an *esprit de corps* among the pupils of his underworld academy, that he is nothing short of creative. With a socially acceptable curriculum, what a progressive headmaster he might have been!

Fagin, corrupter of youth and menace to society, is like Dickens himself, an Inimitable. That the novelist has endowed him with such verve and individuality somewhat weakens our revulsion at the darker portrait of a "loathsome reptile, engendered in slime . . . crawling forth by night."

On one occasion Dickens even permits him a moment of better feeling. Coming upon the sleeping Oliver, Fagin is about to issue a threat and an order for a robbery in the morning.

> The boy was lying, fast asleep . . . so pale with anxiety, and sadness, and the closeness of his prison, that he looked like death . . . in the guise it wears when life has just departed; when a young and gentle spirit has, but an instant, fled to Heaven, and the gross air of the world has not had time to breathe upon the changing dust it hallowed.
>
> "Not now," said the Jew, turning softly away. "Tomorrow. Tomorrow." (Chap. 19)

As Michael Slater has pointed out, "this is almost like the moment in Milton when Satan is staggered and rendered 'stupidly good' by his first sight of Eve in Paradise."[2] Eventually Fagin must admit that his wiles are powerless to corrupt Oliver, who, he concludes, is not "like other boys in the same circumstances. I had no hold *upon* him to make him worse" (Chap. 26).

Such innate goodness residing in an orphan is also seen in Rose Maylie, whose life, like Oliver's, has been clouded by the false assumption of illegitimate birth. To her nature Dickens assigns near divinity, for "if ever angels be for God's good purposes enthroned in mortal forms, they may be, without impiety, supposed to abide in such as hers" (Chap. 29).

In the contrast between good and evil one other character, Nancy, plays an important part. Though linked with Fagin, she is actually his victim, for her enslavement to Sikes holds her in Fagin's den. Because her part in abducting Oliver is carried out under duress and because she becomes his protector and shows physical courage in defying Sikes and Fagin, she is presented sympathetically. Clearly, it is her desperate childhood that has produced the creature who describes herself to Rose Maylie as one "that lives among the thieves, and that never from the first moment . . . on London streets [has] known any better life . . ." (Chap. 40). This cry points up Dickens's indictment of a state which assumes no responsibility for the child.

Nurtured in "the alley and the gutter," Nancy predicts that "they will be [her] death-bed" as well. The remedy, she suggests to the sympathetic Rose, lies in a changed society: ". . . if there was more like you, there would be fewer like me,—there would— there would!" (Chap. 40). But for all this, stern Victorian morality must be served, and Dickens cannot allow Nancy to escape her tragic end. She must atone for guilt through a brutal death at Sikes's hand. But that she may expect divine, if not human, mercy is evident as, with blood streaming from her gashed forehead, she raises Rose's white handkerchief in a symbolic plea to heaven.

It is Nancy's sacrifice which frees Oliver. Because of her murder Sikes is hounded until he accidentally hangs himself; Fagin is captured, brought to trial, and executed; and Monks, forced to renounce his inheritance in favor of his half-brother, migrates to the New World, to perish there as a result of further fraud and knavery. It is a resolution typical of Dickens's early novels, where punishment is meted out to all evildoers.

(Dickens's sympathetic portrayal of Nancy, an early instance of his charitable attitude toward what the Victorians called the "fallen woman," would be followed by a succession of such characters in whom some redemptive spark of decency lingers, as in Martha Endell [DC]. The novelist's preoccupation with this subject was a generating force behind Urania Cottage, the home for wayward women in Shepherd's Bush, which he helped Angela Burdett-Coutts to organize and administer.)

With the evil forces eliminated, the triumphant Oliver will

henceforth live secure in the Brownlow household, surrounded by the love of his surrogate father and his aunt, Rose Maylie (actually Rose Fleming, now discovered to be his dead mother's sister—a characteristic Dickensian twist). The gentle housekeeper, Mrs. Bedwin, and the surgeon who had once tended Oliver's wounds will also be at hand with loving support. To Oliver all this is "like Heaven itself," a world where "everything is quiet and neat and orderly" (Chap. 14)—not surprisingly the three demands Dickens made of his own household.

The plotting of *Oliver Twist* is typical of Dickens's early work— evil characters punished, good ones rewarded. In a plot where everything fits neatly, Nancy becomes the link between opposing forces. Though nominally of Fagin's band, she has redeeming qualities which tie her to Oliver's protectors. She is, as Dickens noted in his 1867 preface, "the soul of goodness in things evil." She demonstrates "God's truth, for it is the truth He leaves in such depraved and miserable breasts; the hope yet lingering there; the last fair drop of water at the bottom of the weed-choked well."

It is pointless to argue, as some critics have done, that a child of Oliver's workhouse background and prolonged contact with brutality and crime would hardly have the gentle speech and ways to engage the admiration of those who deliver him. But precisely because his goodness is innate he emerges unblemished from his rough background. His speech, idealized to be sure, represents that inborn goodness which can withstand the powers of darkness: it is an outer manifestation. The "language of Angels," Steven Marcus calls it, Dickens's way of showing "that grace has descended on" Oliver.

In portraying the privations of Oliver, Dickens drew on his own background for germinal ideas. For he had also been cast adrift, had endured in the blacking warehouse the anguish of a condemned soul, and had been introduced in the streets to such sights of wickedness that only providence had saved him from becoming a little vagabond or thief. Was it also his inherent goodness that had saved him? With the parallels too striking to be dismissed, Dickens transmutes his own early woes into the history of an unwanted parish boy, his earliest novel to use a child as its center.[3] In so doing he transforms his personal bitter-

ness into a social document to jolt an apathetic public into awareness of the lot of countless Olivers.

In nearly every novel after *Oliver Twist* orphans or demi-orphans occupy prominent positions. In *Nicholas Nickleby* (1838–39)
Nicholas and Kate have lost their father before the novel opens;
and Smike, motherless, has been separated from his father in
early childhood. In *The Old Curiosity Shop* (1840–41) Little Nell,
having lost both parents, wanders from place to place with her
incompetent grandfather; and Kit Nubbles shares the family
burdens with his widowed mother. In *Barnaby Rudge* (1841) Edward Chester is motherless, as is Hugh; Barnaby, with his father
in hiding, has only his mother to look after him. In *Martin Chuzzlewit* (1843–44) young Martin, Mary Graham, and Tom and
Ruth Pinch have all lost both parents. *Dombey and Son* (1846–48)
has as its principals the motherless Florence and Paul Dombey,
and Walter Gay, who has lost both parents. Representing opposite ends of the scale, both Edith Granger and Alice Marwood are
fatherless. The largest cluster of orphans or demi-orphans appears in *David Copperfield* (1849–50). Without either parent are
David, Ham, Little Emily, the Micawbers' "Orfling," Traddles,
Clara Copperfield, Martha Endell, Rosa Dartle, and Dora Spenlow. Annie Strong, Steerforth, and Uriah Heep have lost their
fathers; Agnes Wickfield has been motherless since early childhood. In *Bleak House* (1852–53) Esther Summerson, Ada Clare,
and Richard Carstone are parentless. If Jo, the miserable crossing sweeper, has any parents, they have abandoned him, as has
society. Without either parent in *Little Dorrit* (1855–57) are Tattycoram and Maggie; Tip, Fanny, and Amy Dorrit have only a
proud but ineffectual father, a longtime Marshalsea prisoner. In
A Tale of Two Cities (1859) two important characters, Sidney Car-
ton and Charles Darnay, are orphans; and Lucie Manette has
only her long absent father. Both Pip and Biddy in *Great Expectations* (1861) are parentless, and in *Our Mutual Friend* (1864–65)
John Harmon has neither parent. In the unfinished *Edwin Drood*
(1970) Neville and Helena Lawless are orphans. That orphans
and half-orphans figure in every novel from first to last (in *Pickwick Papers* Sam Weller is motherless) clearly indicates Dickens's
obsession with the theme of the homeless child cast adrift in an
alien world.

With such an abundance of examples to draw from, any further consideration of Dickens's long preoccupation with orphans must necessarily be selective. Because *David Copperfield* is in part autobiographical, with actual incidents and situations either faithfully recorded or romantically transformed, it is an obvious choice. Of all the novels, moreover, it is the most persuasive in its evidence that Dickens identified his own boyhood with that of children victimized by an unfeeling society. Like David, whose happiness ends abruptly when the Murdstones take over, young Charles had also lost all semblance of a normal home life when he went to work at the blacking warehouse. Because he had felt betrayed when his mother wished him to continue at the warehouse after his father's release from prison, Dickens may have suggested through the death of Clara Copperfield that his own mother, whom he had idolized in early childhood, was now dead to his love.

In his identification with orphans, Dickens used *David Copperfield* not only to record and transform his own experience—he, too, had "felt an orphan in the wide world" (Chap. 9)—but also to emphasize the role of the surrogate parent. This topic was to receive its fullest treatment in the novel he called his "favourite child."

After his mother's death David's comforter is Peggotty. Having given him loving care from infancy, she has already become a mother figure and now functions as a substitute parent. But all too soon her dismissal terminates the relationship. Murdstone, for whom David has conceived an Oedipal distrust ("he seemed to be very fond of my mother—I am afraid I liked him none the better for that—"), then discharges his responsibility by sending the boy to Murdstone and Grinby's Warehouse, Blackfriars. (The very name "Murdstone" is a significant transparency: by his hardness and actual abuse of David, Murdstone has already killed any kinship the boy might have developed with him. With his view of children as little vipers—a view generally held by Evangelical creeds—and his cruel discipline he is a foil to the benevolent surrogates in this novel, whose humanity appears all the nobler in contrast.)

Although the Micawbers function as surrogate parents while David lodges with them, their chaotic household with its financial crises does not qualify as a secure refuge for an orphaned boy. Their home is, rather, an accurate transcription of Dickens's own after his family moved to Camden Town. As generally agreed, Wilkins Micawber displays all the weakness and eccentricity of John Dickens himself—his ineptness in financial matters, his elasticity in countering reversals with sanguine expectations, and his rhetorical flourishes in dramatizing any new threat to his security. Treated both satirically and whimsically, the Micawber episodes become cathartic as Dickens relives his own early trauma. In spite of his shortcomings, Micawber is, in the main, portrayed with the playful serio-comic detachment which Dickens could not always summon up in regard to his own father.

Unlike the Micawbers, Aunt Betsey does fill a significant place in shaping David's character. Brusque and taciturn on first acquaintance, unabashed in her contempt for men in general, eccentric in her forays against trespassing donkeys, the surrogate mother that emerges from beneath her deceptive surface is one to whom a boy recovering from the privations of childhood can turn as he faces the perplexities of maturation. For all her bluster and professed hatred of boys, she is compassionate and tender as she receives the runaway David into her home.

Until his rescue by Aunt Betsey, David had undergone a succession of shocks: his mother's marriage to the stony-hearted Murdstone, his brutalizing period at Murdstone and Grinby's, and his terrifying encounters on the Dover road. At every turn the adult world had taken advantage of the unsuspecting child: he was made the unwitting butt of jokes by Murdstone and a companion; he was duped by a waiter who consumed most of his dinner and ale; he was intimidated, threatened, cheated, and robbed on his journey to Aunt Betsey's. Speaking for Dickens, the adult David would reflect that a child's "simple confidence" must too early be exchanged for "worldly wisdom" (Chap. 5).

The hour Aunt Betsey takes her vagabond nephew under her care she begins to minister to his comfort. Once he is bathed and swaddled like an infant, he may be said to be reborn, as Q. D. Leavis points out.[4] He must next be schooled in preparation for a useful future. As he matures, his aunt's respect deepens along with her love, and she appeals to his judgment at the onset of her apparent financial ruin. But she must test him: how will he accept poverty? Thus she says nothing about the thousand pounds she has secreted against an emergency. True to the ideals she has instilled, David passes the test and adjusts to his circumstances.

When he succumbs to the first raptures of romantic love, his aunt shrewdly grasps the situation: he is running after "wax dolls." He is "blind, blind, blind" in choosing a bride with the failings of his pretty lost mother, "a most unworldly, most unfortunate baby," a "poor little fool" (Chap. 14). Yet, like a wise parent, she refrains from interfering. Later when the child bride proves unfit for marriage and David sees that "there can be no disparity in marriage like unsuitability of mind and purpose," Aunt Betsey does not take sides. "Your future is between you two," she counsels; "you are to work it out yourselves" (Chap. 44).

After Dora's death it is Aunt Betsey who cleverly steers David to marital happiness by suggesting that Agnes has a secret "attachment" and is about to be married, a shock which rouses him into fulfilling the prophecy as his aunt had hoped (Chap. 62).

In every way Aunt Betsey has fulfilled the role of an ideal mother—compassionate but not blindly sentimental, forthright but not domineering. She has helped David to achieve manhood and to discipline his heart. He owes her everything and vows that "my poor mother could not have loved me better, or studied more to make me happy" (Chap. 37).

The benefits of the relationship have not been David's alone. Aunt Betsey has also been transformed. Once seen by the townspeople as "gruffish . . . and comes down on you sharp," she has since mellowed. Once more, as in the relationship between Florence Dombey and her stepmother, Edith, Dickens affirms his belief in the child's ennobling influence on the parent. At its best, the relationship is a reciprocal one.

Somewhat less reciprocal, however, is the relationship between Aunt Betsey and her confused, gray-haired child, Mr. Dick, whom she has saved from confinement in a mental institution. True, the presence in the house of a man (though in years only) may compensate somewhat for the errant husband who had once made her life miserable. True also, she habitually requests Mr. Dick's advice and praises his occasional spurts of common sense ("Mr. Dick sets us all right"). She introduces him as a friend "on whose judgment I rely" (Chap. 14). This shows not so much actual reliance as maternal tact: it is her wise way of bringing out the best by fostering a sense of self-worth in her charge. He must be made to feel that he occupies a valued place in the home, an assurance to children of whatever age or mental status.

Dickens's portrait of Aunt Betsey may be the fulfillment of an unconscious wish. After his own mother had alienated his affections, he might well have turned to such a substitute, had one been available. An Aunt Betsey might even have steered him toward the "dear presence" of an Agnes, with whom there would have been "no disparity of mind and purpose." David found maternal love and guidance in a surrogate mother; Charles Dickens fought his way to manhood alone.

On a lower social scale than Aunt Betsey, Daniel Peggotty is nonetheless fully as admirable. A hard-working lobster fisherman, he shares his ingeniously arranged boat house with his adopted family: a widow and two orphans, his niece, little Emily, and his nephew, Ham. Beneath his rough exterior and his ungrammatical speech resides a gentle, understanding man whose devotion to his adopted family surpasses that of most parents. He is, as George Ford says in his introduction to the Riverside Edition of *David Copperfield*, "the most ideally paternal figure in the book." Toward Emily his tenderness is especially fervent. In Ham he sees her strong and honest protector ("no wrong can touch my Em'ly while so be that man lives" (Chap. 21), an ironic observation in view of later events. Like a wise parent, though, he will not force the union of these two, however much he may wish it. Emily's choice is to be her own; she is "to be as free as a little bird" (Chap. 21). Nonetheless, her uncle's obvious wish influences her acquiescence.

That paternal love for Emily has become the mainspring of Mr. Peggotty's existence is demonstrated by his physical reaction when he learns of her flight ("his hair wild, his face and lips quite white, and blood trickling down his bosom"). Against Steerforth, her seducer, he now vents his fury: "I would have drownded *him*, as I'm a livin' soul, if I had had one thought of what was in him!" (Chap. 31). But for Emily he has no words of condemnation, no bitterness because of the pain she has caused him, only compassion. "I'm a going to find my poor niece in her shame, and bring her back," he vows. "No one stop me!" So begins his long search for "the pride and hope of my 'art—her that I'd have died for, and would die for now." That her humiliation has been his humiliation, her suffering his suffering, is clear from his report after he finds her: "when I heerd her voice, as I had heerd at home so playful—and see her humbled, as it might be in the dust our Saviour wrote in with his blessed hand—I felt a wound go to my 'art, in the midst of all its thankfulness" (Chap. 51).

However moving the old man's account of this reunion, the modern reader may well have some reservations about the following passage: "But, all night long, her arms has been about my neck; and her head has laid heer . . ." (Chap. 51). Although meant to portray a normal paternal-filial relationship, such close and prolonged contact between adults seems rather suggestive. Was Dickens so carried away by the emotion inherent in his own creation that he failed to recognize possible implications? Whatever his response, this episode draws the curtain on Emily's sordid interlude with Steerforth and prepares us to accept her regeneration during a life of good works in Australia. But, by denying her the happiness of marriage and children, Dickens makes her atone for her past mistakes.

Although Mr. Peggotty has never condemned Emily for bringing disgrace to his name, his migrating with her to Australia, "where no one can't reproach my darling" (Chap. 51), blots out the stain. Mr. Peggotty's deep commitment to his prodigal child elicits one of Dickens's eloquent exhortations: "Aye, Emily, beautiful and drooping, cling to him, with the utmost trust of thy bruised heart; for he has clung to thee, with all the might of his great love" (Chap. 57). Such devotion is fittingly summed up in the farewell message Ham asks David to relay to his uncle: "— will you give him the lovingest duty and thanks of the orphan, as he was ever more than a father to?" (Chap. 51).

However wide the social gap between Aunt Betsey and Mr. Peggotty, there is no difference in the quality of their devotion to their orphans. For Dickens the good parent transcends class. In *David Copperfield* two widely dissimilar social levels are interwoven as the principal surrogate parents display a common nobility. An early link is the faithful Peggotty; through her David is introduced to Mr. Peggotty, Emily, and Ham. Ironically, he in turn brings Steerforth to Yarmouth and unwittingly initiates the events that shatter Mr. Peggotty's happiness. Through Emily's disgrace the Peggotty home has been despoiled, as is symbolized by its physical destruction during the storm at Yarmouth. Into this tightly knit plot Dickens deftly weaves all the other threads: the Strongs, Miss Mowcher, Mrs. Steerforth and Rosa Dartle, and the Heeps, as well as the Micawbers—all are in some way connected with one or both of the surrogate parent-child pairs. And the whole is neatly held together by Aunt Betsey and Mr. Peggotty.

In *Great Expectations,* which may be paired with *David Copperfield* as the only other Dickens novel to use the first-person narrator throughout, the sustaining power of love again resides in a simple man of the lower classes. Joe Gargery is a "mild, good-natured, sweet-tempered, easy-going, foolish" fellow (Chap. 2), actually "a larger species of child" (Chap. 5). Uneducated, his speech interspersed with colorful crudities, he appears at his best in his forge, where he combines strength with gentleness, "like the steelhammer, that can crush a man or pat an egg-shell" (Chap. 18). To him Pip is further bound by the abuses both must endure from his sister, Joe's wife, who has brought the orphan up "by hand." Her appearance reflects her hardness of character. Tall and bony, she wears a "coarse apron" with an "impregnable bib in front . . . stuck full of pins and needles" (Chap. 2). Because of her harsh red skin Pip wonders whether she washes "with a nutmeg grinder instead of soap." Her "trenchant way of cutting bread and butter" further points up her lack of tenderness.

To her, Pip is a nuisance and a burden, giving rise to self-pitying complaints, which instill in him a sense of guilt. He is also beset by fear, for she threatens him with stinging applications of the "Tickler" and sends him to bed in the dark. Had Joe not insisted there was room enough for Pip under their roof, the boy would have been a ward of the parish. Mrs. Joe's cold and repressive treatment places her with the Murdstones in the group of Dickens's surrogates whose brutality contrasts sharply with the generally laudable behavior of his model adoptive parents.

Whenever Pip suffers from his sister's violent moods, Joe shares his misery and would gladly take the punishment upon himself. When his wife humiliates the boy before dinner guests, Joe makes amends by giving him an additional serving of gravy. Because he is a "larger species of child," he can communicate with Pip, as by exchanging winks with him when they are both banished in disgrace to their kitchen corner. "Wot larks!" he exclaims of their amusements and horseplay. As Robert Stange has observed, "Joe emerges as a true parent—the only kind of parent that Dickens could ever fully approve, one that remains a child."[5]

With his childlike quality, moreover, he combines a sense of values, an awareness of right and wrong, as Pip realizes intuitively when he confides some misgivings over having lied after his first visit to Miss Havisham. His shame at being thought common had made him do it, he explains. "Lies is lies," admonishes Joe; "don't you tell no more of 'em, Pip. *That* ain't the way to get out of being common, old chap" (Chap. 9). Later, when Pip is restless and dejected during his apprenticeship at the forge, it is only because of Joe's trust that he does his work and stays on the job ("It was not because I was faithful, but because Joe was faithful that I never ran away and went for a soldier or sailor"). The good done by such a man, Pip finally realizes, is incalculable: "It is not possible to know how far the influence of any amiable honest-hearted duty-doing man flies out into the world; but it is very possible to know how it has touched one's self in going by . . ." (Chap. 14).

That Magwitch also fills the role of surrogate parent is clearly indicated when he tells Pip, "I'm your second father. You're my son—more son to me nor any son" (Chap. 39). So pervasive is his influence that one critic has called it "the fulcrum of the novel's movement."[6] Although his presence in the opening chapters is brief and his later appearance of no great duration, Magwitch has an impact on some crucial stages of Pip's development. Through him the boy's simple set of values will be overturned, his world made topsy-turvy, as is in fact foreshadowed when the convict holds him upside down by his heels in the marshes. During this terrifying encounter Pip is introduced to the criminal world. With his theft of the file and food he actually begins to feel an affinity with the convict. This criminal identity is reinforced when he hopes that the pursuing soldiers will not find their prey. When, following his capture, Magwitch exonerates

Fig. 17.   Taking Leave of Joe, illustration by Marcus Stone, from *Great Expectations*

Pip by assuming the blame for the theft of the file and food, Pip's fellow feeling for the convict increases. It is worth noting here that Magwitch was also an orphan. Society having wronged him, he turned to a life of crime. Pip and Magwitch, both victims of rejection, have an unconscious basis for sympathy.

Though Magwitch will not reappear until much later, Pip is not allowed to forget him, especially after a stranger at the Three Jolly Bargemen leaves him a shining shilling wrapped in two one-pound notes. These, secreted by Mrs. Joe under a pot of dried rose leaves, will remain a "nightmare" to him "many a night and day" (Chap. 10). He is again tormented by guilt when his sister is felled with a convict's leg iron. Because it had been removed with the stolen file, he feels responsible for providing the weapon.

Once in London, to be groomed as a gentleman in preparation for coming into "a handsome property," Pip is still more closely linked with the world of crime when he learns about Jaggers's unsavory cases and visits Newgate Prison. Even his desultory spendthrift mode of life keeps him near the wrong side of the law as he moves ever closer to arrest for debt.

Against this background with its criminal resonance Magwitch, once more a fugitive, is reintroduced. Pip's horror on learning the identity of his benefactor (Chap. 39) parallels his childhood terror on first meeting the convict. The earlier pursuit by the soldiers has its counterpart in the chase on the Thames, where even the surroundings remind Pip of his "own marsh country" (Chap. 54). In a life-and-death struggle on the river Magwitch again grapples with his old foe, the second convict. With this structural symmetry, reinforced by Magwitch's capture and imprisonment, the novel has comes full circle: his property confiscated by the Crown, the convict is once again the penniless fugitive of the marshes. And Pip, having lost his "great expectations," threatened with imprisonment for debt, humbled, broken in health, survives only because the man who took pity on him as a homeless orphan now nurses him back to health. "For, the tenderness of Joe was so beautifully proportioned to my need, that I was like a child in his hands," Pip declares. "He would sit back and talk to me in the old confidence, and with the old simplicity, ... so that I would half believe that all my life since the days in the old kitchen was one of the mental troubles of the fever that was gone" (Chap. 57).

It is not unreasonable to regard Pip's collapse and coma as the symbolic death of the character created by Magwitch. With his recovery he emerges a new man. Gone are his false pride, his shame over his humble background, his ambition to be a gentleman. True gentility, he now realizes, resides in an unselfish respect for others. As Biddy had once told him, a true gentleman fulfills his place in the world and shows consideration for others —an accurate description of Joe Gargery. It is singularly fitting that such a man should preside over the regeneration of Pip.

Pip's character, then, has undergone developments directly traceable to his two surrogate fathers. In early boyhood he absorbs the noble principles of Joe. When the Magwitch influence pushes these aside, Pip heads toward moral and financial ruin. Then, after his illness and spiritual baptism, he returns to his boyhood values. His life, then, has been dominated by two contesting forces: the underworld (the convicts, Jaggers's unsavory clients, the threat of his own imprisonment) and Joe's forge with its wholesome emphasis on honesty and work. Although Magwitch nearly destroys Pip in the attempt to make a gentleman of him, he eventually accomplishes exactly that. For, once Pip realizes how much Magwitch has risked for him, his revulsion for the convict gives way to pity, crowned finally by affection. Because he can now show feeling for this uncouth man of low station, he has truly become a gentleman. Ironically, then, when Magwitch, mortally injured, tells him, "I've seen my boy, and *he can be a gentleman without me*" [italics mine] (Chap. 54), he unwittingly points up the only real good that has come from their association.

The false values inherent in Magwitch's efforts to penetrate the social barrier for Pip apply also to Miss Havisham, who lets Pip anticipate gentlemanly status from her hand. Having been jilted on her wedding day, Miss Havisham, like Magwitch, is a victim who seeks redress. She has become obsessed with bringing up her ward, the proud and bewitching Estella, to break men's hearts—specifically, Pip's. It is significant that both Magwitch and Miss Havisham illustrate how the manipulation of a child to redress personal grievances recoils upon the adults. Here, too, is another instance of Dickens's effective plotting in that Pip's two expectations, amatory and monetary, both focus on a single source, Magwitch's daughter Estella.

Dickens's abiding interest in the surrogate parent may be documented further with examples from other novels. In *Dombey and Son,* for instance, Solomon Gills concentrates his hopes on Walter Gay, the orphaned nephew for whom he makes a home. In *Bleak House* John Jarndyce, a benevolent bachelor, charges himself with the support of three orphans as he tries to unsnarl the complexities of their chancery suit. For the pathetic Richard Carstone he assumes full parental responsibility by attempting to straighten out his ruined life, generously condoning his instability and unjust suspicions. For Esther Summerson he has been the "best of fathers" (II, 36). (There is a curious ambiguity in this surrogate-parent-*cum*-lover relationship.)

Something further needs to be said about Esther, whose illegitimacy Dickens used to condemn a particularly callous and uncharitable attitude of Victorian society, one which fostered a conviction of inferiority in children born out of wedlock. Branded with their parents' transgressions, these children developed a sense of guilt and shame. On her birthday Esther's godmother tells her, "It would have been far better, little Esther, that you had no birthday; that you had never been born!" (I, 3). On a later birthday she is further admonished: ". . . unfortunate girl, orphaned and degraded from the first of these evil anniversaries, pray daily that the sins of others be not visited upon your head, according to what is written" (I, 3). By contrast, Jarndyce, who fosters Esther's self-worth by giving her the highest place in his home, represents a commendable but minor segment of society.

That Dickens's distaste for the prevailing attitude toward illegitimacy was of long standing is borne out in *Oliver Twist.* Here Rose Maylie, burdened by guilt before she learns the truth about her birth, serves as his mouthpiece: ". . . there is a stain upon my name, which the world visits on innocent heads." It is this "stain" which now prevents her accepting a proposal of marriage: "I will carry it into no blood but my own; and the reproach shall rest on me alone" (Chap. 35). On a later occasion, when Monks refers to

Oliver as "bastard," Dickens has Brownlow challenge his use of a label meant to degrade an innocent victim: "It reflects disgrace on no one living, except you who use it" (Chap. 51).

In Dickens's last completed novel, *Our Mutual Friend,* even Betty Higden, though so poor as to lie under the constant threat of the workhouse, is a surrogate parent. She has taken in Johnny, her dead daughter's son, and Sloppy, a love child "found in the streets." (Obviously the Victorian attitude toward illegitimacy does not color her relationship with Sloppy.) So long as noble men and women open their hearts to orphans, Dickens implies, society is given a pattern to follow.

Admittedly, not all of Dickens's surrogate parents vibrate with love and moral purpose toward their charges. Fagin, as we have seen, corrupts his boys and insures their ultimate imprisonment and death on the gallows, even as he fills the role of adoptive father. No less reprehensible is the brutal schoolmaster Squeers in *Nicholas Nickleby.* Unlike Fagin he must make a public show of assumed paternal care in order to insure his livelihood. Thus, upon the unexpected intrusion of a prospective client, he suddenly changes his tactics toward the weeping child he has just brutally knocked to the floor. "You are leaving your friends," he tells him tenderly, "but you will have a father in me, my dear, and a mother in Mrs. Squeers" (Chap. 4). "To them boys," he explains, his wife is "more than a mother, . . . ten times more. She does things for them boys . . . that I don't believe half the mothers going, would do for their own sons" (Chap. 8). Such ironic boasts need only to be measured against the misery of Dotheboys Hall, where unhealthy, half-starved boys are fed on "potskimmings" and carrion; where Bolder, "incorrigible young scoundrel," is cruelly thrashed because of his warts; where Smike, through years of privation and repression, has become physically and mentally stunted.

Schoolmasters, it seems, did not generally win Dickens's endorsement as surrogate parents. Influenced by recollections of the incompetence and cruelty of the headmaster at his own Wellington House Academy, the novelist made him the original of the obnoxious Creakle of Salem House Academy, a man who delighted "in cutting at the boys, which was like the satisfaction of a craving appetite," an "incapable brute, who had no more right to be possessed of the great trust he held, than to be the Lord High Admiral, or Commander-in-Chief—in either of which capacities it is probable that he would have done infinitely less mischief" (*DC,* Chap. 7). Though not guilty of such brutality and incompetence, Dr. Blimber *(DS)* must be faulted for putting his boys through a system of cramming. In his "great hothouse" a "forcing apparatus" was "incessantly at work." Boys "blew before their time" and, having " 'gone through' everything," like Toots, "suddenly left off blowing one day, and remained . . . a mere stalk" (Chap. 11).

With Bradley Headstone *(OMF)* the shortcomings are of another sort. Ashamed of his humble origin, he was determined to rise in the social scale through his learning. But his education had not enlarged his mental breadth, for "his mind had been a place of mechanical stowage" and "he always seemed to be uneasy lest anything should be missing from his mental warehouse . . ." (II, 1). With such a self-centered and restricted vision of his pedagogical role, he not surprisingly influenced his star pupil, Charley Hexam, to develop into a proud and selfish young man who later turned on his own master.

That surrogates can be as deficient as biological parents is indeed borne out by the examples just cited. But even with well-intentioned surrogates, efforts to provide a home for an orphan sometimes miscarry, as when the Meagleses *(LD)* adopt Tattycoram. Implicit in this failure is Meagles's class consciousness, apparent when he curries favor with the Barnacles: "He was striving after something that did not belong to him, he was not himself" (I, 17). His emphasis on social status explains why Tattycoram, whose "ways" are considered "a little wide of ours" (I, 2), is received as a lesser family member, performing the duties of a maid for Pet, the Meagleses' only child. Even the grotesque name by which they address her (against her expressed wish) is a slight, for it emphasizes her background, the foundling hospital in Coram Fields, from which the Meagleses procured her. When Tattycoram seeks equality and love in a refuge with Miss Wade, Dickens again demonstrates his awareness of the dark undercurrents in the human psyche. There can be no doubt that Meagles is dealing with a lesbian when he accuses Miss Wade of taking "a perverted delight in making a sister-woman as wretched as she is

(I am old enough to have heard of such)." His final admonition is unequivocal: "I warn her [Tattycoram] against you, and I warn you against yourself" (I, 27). It could be argued that Dickens introduces Miss Wade as another example of how the victim of neglect may fall under sinister influences. Having had no parental guidance during her formative years, she has been molded by unnatural forces in her environment.

Returning to Dickens's admirable surrogates, how do they fulfill the requirements of responsible parents? Of first importance is their genuine love for their orphans. Mr. Brownlow, the Maylies, Aunt Betsey, Mr. Peggotty, Joe Gargery—all offer a sincere affection which can only be returned in full measure. Their love manifests itself in tangible ways. In the Brownlow home Oliver lacks nothing to make him happy: his own attractive room, good clothes, devoted nursing care. For David, Aunt Betsey draws heavily on her savings to see him through school and prepare him for a profession. Though more limited in his means, Mr. Peggotty remodels an old barge to make a comfortable home for his orphans. For Joe, who regards Pip more as a companion than a responsibility, happiness consists in fully sharing all he owns.

In addition to providing their orphans with material necessities, these foster parents build the character of their charges. Mr. Brownlow scatters the "thriving seeds" of all he wishes Oliver to become. Aunt Betsey plants suggestions that eventually help David to see how his "undisciplined heart" has blocked his happiness. Joe Gargery, merely by being himself, a true gentleman, brings about the regeneration of Pip and sends him forth into a life of genuine meaning. Not one of these surrogate parents resorts to threats, offensive moralizing, or bribes for performance of duty. It is enough that each one's example inspires confidence and points the way to a fulfilling life.

Because they are dedicated to helping those least able to help themselves, the young victims of social injustice, Dickens's ideal surrogate parents are among his noblest characters. They give their orphans a refuge of love and security in an uncertain and hostile world, an escape from the wasteland of crime and punishment. Having observed too many failures in nineteenth-century parenthood, Dickens offered these models to an irresponsible state. Only by accepting its parental obligations could a nation escape inevitable disaster. "Judgement for an evil thing is many times delayed some day or two, some century or two, but it is as sure as life, it is as sure as death!" Carlyle had warned in *Past and Present* (I, ii). It remained for Dickens to reinforce this warning by addressing a larger audience through his fiction.

Chapter 6

"An Outcast from a Living Parent's Love"

"... for not an orphan in the wide world can be so deserted as the child who is an outcast from a living parent's love."

Dombey and Son (Chap. 24)

In contrast to those substitute parents who devote themselves to the welfare of their adopted orphans, most of Dickens's biological parents are found wanting. Though numerous examples could be cited, three novels, one each from the early, middle, and final period of his career, portray the cruelty of parents who withhold their love and ignore their children's feelings: *Barnaby Rudge* (1841), *Dombey and Son* (1846–48), and *Our Mutual Friend* (1864–65).

Typical is John Willet *(BR)*, the domineering landlord of the Maypole, who still treats his son, a "broad-shouldered strapping young fellow of twenty," like a little boy. "My father!" protests the frustrated Joe. "Will he never think me man enough to take care of myself!" (Chap. 22). Before the patrons of the public house he endures frequent insults to his manhood. "When your opinion's wanted," his father adds after ordering him to be silent, "you give it. When you're spoke to, you speak" (Chap. 1). So "despotic" is John Willet, with such "high mightiness and majesty" does he fill his paternal office, that his son is occasionally goaded into open rebellion. "I cannot bear the contempt that your treating me in the way you do, brings upon me from others every day," he complains. He sees himself as a "bye-word all over Chigwell" and warns that when he is finally driven to break his degrading bonds, his father will be solely responsible (Chap. 3).

"Bullied, badgered, worried, fretted, and brow-beaten" (Chap.

30), repeatedly humiliated, Joe escapes his frustration by joining the army. For John Willet the disappearance of his son is a precursor to ruin. Never having shown Joe any fatherly affection, having regarded him simply as a useful chattel, he now begins to sense his loss. The destruction of the Maypole by the Gordon Rioters climaxes his misfortunes and leaves him irreparably shock-damaged. When his son returns from America after having lost an arm in defense of Savannah, their earlier positions are reversed: it is the father who must now be treated like a child as he tries to fathom the mystery of Joe's empty sleeve; and the son addresses him like a father answering a small boy's questions. It is a compelling instance of retribution: the father, indirectly responsible for his son's physical crippling, will now end his days as a mental cripple.

On a higher social scale *Barnaby Rudge* represents yet another study of father-son friction when Sir John Chester insists that his son, Edward, renounce his love for Emma Haredale and marry a rich heiress who can replenish the squandered family fortune. Although Sir John professes to regard the relationship between father and son as "positively quite a holy kind of bond" (Chap. 12), this is sheer hypocrisy; for Sir John has hitherto ignored this bond in declaring that a son, "unless he is old enough to be a companion," can only be a "restraint upon his father" and his father "a restraint upon him." So they make each other mutually uncomfortable. For this reason Edward has spent most of his boyhood at a distant school. Had he been "awkward and overgrown," his father assures him, "I should have exported you to some distant part of the world" (Chap. 15). (The importance he attaches to appearance, dress, and certain niceties of deportment suggests that he may have been modeled on Lord Chesterfield.)

Although Edward sensibly suggests that they allow a reasonable period to elapse before facing this painful topic of his marriage plans, Sir John, slyly shifting his strategy, reveals that his elegant style of living and his inability to exist without certain refinements have brought on ruinous debts. Shocked by this disclosure, Edward feels like a villain for having won the love of Emma Haredale when he can offer her only poverty.

Sir John then resorts to treachery by secretly trying to convince Emma that her affections have been trifled with. This he follows up, when Edward senses a change in her attitude, with the suggestion that Emma had been interested only in his money. "The lady being poor and you poor also," he argues, "there is an end to the matter." When Edward remains loyal to Emma, however, Sir John threatens to disown him. "It is sad," Edward observes, "when a son, proffering [his father] his love and duty in their best and truest sense, finds himself repelled at every turn, and forced to disobey." As a final and, to him, almost unbelievable rejection, his father orders him to "go to the Devil" (Chap. 32) and return to the parental roof no more.

Even more reprehensible than John Willet, who bullies his son and violates his dignity, Sir John Chester cruelly rejects his son's affection. The role of parent is repugnant to him; indeed, he even refuses to be called "father." "For Heaven's sake don't call me by that obsolete and ancient name," he orders Edward. "Have some regard for delicacy. Am I grey, or wrinkled, do I go on crutches, have I lost my teeth, that you adopt such a mode of address? Good God, how very coarse!" (Chap. 32). Almost his last words, before he is mortally wounded in a duel, show how completely he has abandoned his fatherhood: "Poor fool! . . . he [Edward] is no longer son of mine" (Chap. 81). He represents a class of parents whom Dickens found intolerable, those who seek profit at the expense of their children, for whom they feel no affection.

Still more despicable is Sir John's conduct toward Hugh, his bastard son by a gypsy. Chester has so manipulated him in devious schemes that he has been utterly perverted to crime. Even when the father-son kinship is revealed as Hugh is condemned to the gallows, Chester denies the blood tie and assumes no responsibility for neglecting and corrupting his natural son. Hugh is the victim of his father, against whom he fittingly invokes a final curse: "What . . . should teach me—me, born as I was born, and reared as I have been reared—to hope for any mercy in this hardened, cruel, unrelenting place! . . . On the head of that man, who, in his conscience, owns me for his son, I leave the wish that he may never sicken on his bed of down, but die a violent death as I do now, and have the night-wind for his only mourner" (Chap. 77). Chester's violent death in a duel appropriately fulfills this curse. In the treatment of his two sons he symbolizes a society that has denied its children.

A still more villainous father is Rudge, a murderer whose crime was responsible for the prenatal damage to his half-witted Barnaby. The son having been told that his fugitive father is dead, the two clash as strangers on the road one dark night, a situation strikingly Oedipal. Later Barnaby learns the identity of his opponent in this encounter and makes filial overtures, but is repulsed by a hard, unfeeling man.

In *Barnaby Rudge* a total lack of love characterizes the three fathers. They are either wantonly cruel like Rudge, self-serving in their craftiness like Chester, or insensitive like Willet. In *Dombey and Son* another motive, family pride, underlies parental cruelty. Here the plot focuses on a father who views his children as property, then is spiritually redeemed through a daughter's unselfish love. Dombey represents the Victorian class which equated England's greatness with material prosperity. His sole objective is to expand the family shipping firm against the time when his son will be old enough to become an active partner. As a person Dombey is a nonentity, a cipher who cares nothing for literature: his "bookcase, glazed and locked, repudiated all familiarities," its "unattainable treasure" suitably guarded by a bronze bust of Mr. Pitt (Chap. 5), a symbol of economic ruthlessness. For music he has no taste, not recognizing the most familiar strains. Of games he is ignorant, never having occasion to resort to such trifling play.

Completely absorbed in the future of his firm, he concentrates all his hopes on his small son, Paul, valued only as a future asset. He deprives him of his childhood by rushing him through stages of development that should come naturally. For Florence, his older child, he harbors only cold indifference. As a girl she has no more value in his business than "a piece of base coin that couldn't be invested" (Chap. 1). Even as she looks for the first time at her new brother, whose birth has taken her mother's life, she is rebuffed with a warning not to touch him.

Before long, Dombey's cold indifference to Florence turns to irritation; for he has seen love and understanding developing between her and her brother, and he feels excluded. That little

Paul turns to Florence and also enjoys his seaside intimacy with Old Glubb is evidence that he is starved for love. Dombey would ignore Florence's existence altogether if he could: "She troubled his peace. He would have preferred to put her idea aside altogether, if he had known how" (Chap. 3). Actually, he does momentarily blot out an awareness of her when he makes a Freudian slip in writing "beloved and only child" for the inscription on the tablet over Paul's grave.

Though he grows even more distant to Florence in his bereavement, his memories poisoned by the knowledge that his dead son had preferred her to himself, his daughter continues her efforts to penetrate the barrier between them. Herself grief-stricken by the loss of her brother, she understands Dombey's misery, his blighted hopes. She tries to fill the void in his life, to share his loneliness, to wait on him tenderly. Nightly she crouches on the cold floor outside his bedroom, listening to his breathing, yearning for an opportunity to comfort him. Once, finding the door open and "urged on by the love within her, and the trial they [have] undergone together, but not shared," she glides in. But the face Dombey turns on her, "without one touch of tenderness and pity," terrifies her; she freezes before it and looks at him "as if stricken into stone." Here Dickens interpolates a series of rhetorical questions that bare her father's inner conflict. Does Dombey see her as "his own successful rival" to his son's affection? Have "a mad jealousy and withered pride" poisoned "remembrances that should have endeared and made her precious to him"? Is it "gall to him to look upon her in her beauty and her promise" as he thinks of his dead boy? As he takes Florence by the arm to eject her, his hand is "cold, and loose, and scarcely closed upon her" (Chap. 18). Seeing the futility of trying to touch his heart, Florence drops her head "upon her hands with one prolonged low cry." She knows herself outcast, alienated. The dream of winning her father's love is over. As the scene rushes to an awesome conclusion, Dickens interpolates an admonition with the force of an incantation: "Let him remember it in that room, years to come. . . . Let him remember it . . ." (Chap. 18).

Dombey does indeed remember—cannot, in fact, forget Florence's face as it keeps reappearing in fancy during his train ride

Fig. 18. "Let him remember it in that room, years to come!" illustration by Hablôt K. Browne (Phiz) from *Dombey and Son*

to Leamington. "One child . . . gone, and one child left," he reflects. Why has death robbed him of "the one object of his hope"
instead of her? Unwelcome to him from the first, she is an
"aggravation of his bitterness now." Her "loving and innocent
face" keeps rising before him, but with no "softening or winning
influence." He has "rejected the angel" and taken up "with the
tormenting spirit crouching in his bosom" (Chap. 20). In time the
image of his daughter's face will blend with Paul's and Dombey
will soften toward her, seeing her by "a clearer and brighter
light, not bending over that child's pillow as a rival . . . but as the
spirit of his home . . ." (Chap. 35). In portraying Dombey's inner
conflict, Dickens wants it understood that his regeneration, when
it comes, will not be unmotivated.

While visiting friends at Fulham, Florence overhears what confirms her long suspicions: her father has never wanted her.
Unobserved, she listens as a sympathetic woman explains to a
small niece that Florence's father "cares little for her, very seldom sees her, never was kind to her, and now quite shuns and
avoids her." A final comment plunges Florence into prolonged
and bitter weeping: ". . . for not an orphan in the wide world can
be so deserted as the child who is an outcast from a living parent's love" (Chap. 24). Florence is virtually an orphan now in
her own home.

At this point Dickens introduces a development that shows his
grasp of an important principle in child psychology: when harsh
reality becomes unbearable a sensitive child seeks escape in fanta-
sy. Florence fancies how, had she been a favorite child, she and
her father would have visited her brother's grave together, how
he would have stressed their "common hope and trust in God."
At other times she counsels herself to be patient, to prepare for
a day when she will "win [her father] to a better knowledge of his
only child." At her books, her music, her work, in her morning
walks and nightly prayers, her "engrossing aim" is to be "profi-
cient enough" to please him when at last they become companions. As repeatedly throughout this novel, Dickens must inject his
personal response: "Strange study for a child, to learn the road
to a hard parent's heart!" (Chap. 23).

Through an ironic combination of circumstances that hard
heart grows even harder after Dombey marries Edith Granger.
Though Florence hopes that her new mother will teach her the

way to win her father's love ("Oh, let me learn from you how to become dearer to Papa"), she encounters his even greater hostility. For Dombey once more sees her as a rival. Just as little Paul had been happiest in her company, so Edith, tormented as "a bought woman" in a loveless marriage, is drawn to her stepdaughter, whose innocence and purity offer her the only relief from a crass domestic relationship. (Here, as in instances cited elsewhere, Dickens again confirms his belief in a child's ennobling influence on an erring adult.) Infuriated by his wife's increasing alienation and her imperious refusal to recognize his superior position ("I am to be deferred to and obeyed," he demands, but her haughty aloofness is a match for his pride), he tries to humiliate her by communicating through his manager some vague threat of reprisal against Florence, who now has become a pawn in the domestic conflict. As this conflict spreads an ominous gloom over the household, Florence remains devoted to her father. Once, while he is recovering from a riding accident, she steals into his room while he is asleep, kisses him, and puts her arm around him. "Awake, doomed man, while she is near," is Dickens's characteristic interpolation. "The time is flitting by; the hour is coming with an angry tread; its foot is in the house. Awake!" (Chap. 43).

But the doomed man takes no heed as he rushes on to catastrophe. When the blow comes—the flight of his wife with his manager, on their anniversary, of all days—he lusts for revenge. Seeing him only as "wronged and deserted," Florence hastens to him, arms outstretched to embrace him, crying, "Oh, dear, dear Papa!" In frenzied rage Dombey strikes her across the face and, as she totters to the marble floor, tells her to follow Edith, with whom he accuses her of having been in league. His wounded pride, his pent-up rage, his sexual frustration have found release in violence. This melodramatic and sentimental scene is followed by a passage more eloquent in its directness and staccato cadence, one of the finest in the novel: "She did not sink at his feet; she did not shut out the sight of him with her trembling hands; she did not utter one word of reproach .... She saw his cruelty, neglect, and hatred .... She saw she had no father upon earth, and ran out, orphaned from his house" (Chap. 47).

Hitherto an "outcast from a living parent's love," Florence is now an outcast from his house as well. With less than a third of the novel remaining, Dickens has yet to show how sacrificial love will eventually transcend the barriers that isolate parent from child. In rapid succession he ties up the plot threads: Florence's temporary refuge with Sol Gills, where she finds warmth and love, followed by her happy marriage to Walter Gay, safely back after having been considered lost at sea; the flight of Dombey's manager, his hideous mutilation and death; Edith's declaration of innocence and self-banishment (though she merely approached the seeming threshold of adultery, Dickens demands her atonement); the collapse of Dombey's firm and his subsequent illness.

With Dombey broken and contrite, alone in his silent house, Dickens deftly recalls an earlier scene. The ruined man wanders into the room where he once rejected Florence's affectionate approaches: "Let him remember it in that room, years to come!" It is the identical admonition of chapter 18, repeated three times. Then follows a highly charged passage, the prose rhythm accentuated by terse parallelisms: "He did remember it. In the miserable night he thought of it; in the dreary day, the wretched dawn, the ghostly, memory-haunted twilight. He did remember it. In agony, in sorrow, in remorse, in despair!" (Chap. 59). For several pages thereafter, with a penetration unmatched in his earlier novels, Dickens portrays Dombey's remorse as his wanderings through the changed house awaken painful memories. In keeping with the earlier characterization of a nonentity, of a man who does not read, cares nothing for music, and plays no games, Dickens again depersonalizes him, showing him in his abject state as a mere reflection in a mirror; it is an image, not a person, that acts and thinks: "Now it rose and walked about . . . . Now, it was looking at the bottom of the door, and thinking. . . . It was thinking that if blood were to trickle that way, and to leak out into the hall, it must be a long time going so far" (Chap. 59). This soul-baring delineation of a ruined merchant prince, tormented by recriminations and suicidal thoughts, ends melodramatically with the appearance of Florence to the rescue.

As already pointed out, Dombey's reclamation is not unmotivated. Something already within finally makes him respond to Florence. For it is her face that has always intruded whenever he has called up an image of his dead son. Inevitably, the vision of Paul's "little figure in a low arm-chair," with its "bright eyes and its old-young face," has been succeeded by "Florence—always Florence" (Chap. 30). And now at last the old ambitions for his firm trouble Dombey no more. For Florence, who is always with him, has at last blended with the visions of Paul. Now Dickens skillfully returns to the irony of his title by having Miss Tox reiterate: "And so Dombey and Son, as I observed upon a certain sad occasion, . . . is indeed a daughter . . . after all" (Chap. 59). As Kathleen Tillotson has pointed out in her excellent chapter on *Dombey and Son (Novels of the Eighteen-Forties),* the real subject of the book is not Dombey and son but Dombey and daughter. In her successful struggle for her father's redemption, Florence has exercised the highest kind of love, one that demands nothing in return. Dickens has aptly entitled chapter 25 "The Study of a Loving Heart."

Although Florence often seems to be waging a battle against insuperable odds for her father's love, Dickens really has not delineated Dombey as an actively bad man. This is borne out by a passage in the 1858 preface: "Mr. Dombey undergoes no violent change . . . . A sense of his injustices is within him all along. The more he represses it, the more unjust he necessarily is . . . . It has been a contest for years, and is only fought out after a long balance of victory." Elsewhere Dickens reminds us that "there are yielding moments in the lives of the sternest and harshest of men, though such men often keep their secrets well" (Chap. 35). Dombey has isolated himself: he is "shut up within himself" (Chap. 20), has "shut out all the world as with a double door of gold" (Chap. 20), and is "shut up in his towering supremacy" (Chap. 51). For all his failings, however, he is an honorable man, as is demonstrated when he insists on selling everything to pay off his creditors.

For John Harmon's father, the dust contractor in *Our Mutual Friend,* there were no such redeeming qualities. Although dead before the novel opens, he has left behind his villainy in the impact it has on his son. As one of Dickens's worst fathers ("tremendous old rascal," "growling old vagabond"), he was a blend of cruelty and caprice. His "highest gratification" came from "anathematizing his nearest relations and turning them out of doors" (I, 2). His wife was his first victim. She was followed by his daughter when she refused to marry a man of his choice because she loved another. Of her death soon after he took no notice.

It was his younger child, John, whose life was most affected by a blighted boyhood. At no time did his father give him counsel or companionship, encourage his interests, or show him any love. Shy and fearful before him, John would linger on the staircase before responding to a summons. He had reason, for his father often indulged a violent temper. The boy's only affection came from the Boffins, his father's manager and housekeeper. Even that ended when he was sent away to be cheaply educated in Brussels. Scantily dressed, shivering in the wind, he had to walk to the steamboat because he had no sixpence for coach fare. It was a tearful parting from the two old friends who had been his only comfort: a last embrace, then a look of agony as he was left "all alone and forgotten" with a pitifully small allowance of five sous.

John was not to see his home again until he was fourteen, and then only because, having heard of his sister's expulsion, he returned to remonstrate with his father. He was promptly "turned out of doors." Dispossessed, he went abroad and eventually made his living as a grape farmer.

As the novel opens, John has returned to England because of a will discovered after his father's death. This document, testimony to the old man's caprice, stipulates that a considerable property—the family home and a veritable mountain range of dust heaps—is to go to the son on one condition: that he marry Bella Wilfer, whom he has never seen and to whom his father was curiously attracted on meeting her only once when she was four. Understandably, John comes back "shrinking from [his] father's money, shrinking from [his] memory, mistrustful of being forced on a mercenary wife" (II, 13). Though no longer present to tyrannize over him, the old man has left legal bonds calculated to maintain his despotic hold. Even from the grave he continues to torment his son.

Unlike John Willet and Mr. Dombey, old Harmon remains cruel and unrelenting. For him there is no regeneration. Like Sir John Chester, he remains devoid of fatherly affection to the end. As a boy John was an "outcast from a living parent's love"; as a man he transcends his early trauma when he finds domestic happiness with a transformed Bella Wilfer. Again it is love that triumphs.

Of the three novels discussed in this chapter, *Dombey and Son* is the most clearly analogous to nineteenth-century England in its treatment of materialistic parents. If, as Jerome Meckier reasons persuasively, Dickens "thought of society's authoritative elements as a kind of parent" and had, consequently, "to redeem the parent who symbolized that body," the reunion of father and daughter does indeed have important implications. With Dombey representing the body of society and Florence the heart and soul, their reunion becomes a symbol of rebirth. Having made a domestic situation a "microcosm for a national one," Dickens implies that a society dominated by greed, insular pride, and ruthless competition can be regenerated only through dedicated love. Thus *Dombey and Son* functions as a fable for its time.

Chapter 7
"The Heir of My Bringing-Up"

"This is the heir of my bringing-up. Sly, cunning, and covetous, he'll not squander my money."

Martin Chuzzlewit (Chap. 11)

For a healthy parent-child relationship Dickens considered character building as essential as the physical comforts and the emotional stability of a home. When children went astray he blamed the parents for either perverting fundamental values or ignoring them altogether. His conviction that parental influences are largely responsible for erring sons and daughters informs several of his novels. Three are especially notable for their penetrating study of the harm done by parents in shaping their children's futures: *Martin Chuzzlewit* (1843–44), *David Copperfield* (1849–50), and *Hard Times* (1854).

In *Martin Chuzzlewit* Anthony has reared his son, Jonas, "on the strictest principles of the main chance" (Chap. 8). The very first words the boy learns to spell are "gain" and "money." For him everything becomes a question of property. So quickly does he devise his own rule for driving a bargain, to "do other men, for they would do you," that his father gloats over having brought up such a sharp son. "*I* taught him. *I* trained him," he boasts. "This is the heir of my bringing-up. Sly, cunning, and covetous, he'll not squander my money. I worked for this; I hoped for this; it has been the great end and aim of my life" (Chap. 11).

But the old man has not anticipated the end results of such training. Having been encouraged to overreach himself, Jonas eventually tests his skill by turning on the very author of his craftiness. With an eye to inheriting the family fortunes intact, he

108

subjects his father to such austere economies as unheated rooms and insufficient food. Finally, impatient with waiting for his inheritance, he plans to poison his father. Although Anthony learns of this plot in time to circumvent it, he remorsefully admits his responsibility for Jonas's degeneracy. "This crime began with me," he laments. "It began when I taught him to be covetous of what I had to leave, and made the expectation of it his great business! . . . It's a dreadful thing to have my own child thirsting for my death. . . . I have sown, and I must reap" (Chap. 51). As if to emphasize Anthony's responsibility for Jonas's corruption, old Chuffy adds, "Your own son," then, significantly, reflects, "his own son."

To reinforce the thesis that parental example and precept must be charged with molding a child's character, Dickens explains in his preface that Jonas, having been "admired for that which made him hateful, and justified from his cradle in cunning, treachery, and avarice," becomes the "legitimate issue of the father upon whom those vices are seen to recoil." That they recoil "upon that old man, in his unhonoured age, is not a mere piece of poetical justice"; it is the "extreme exposition of direct truth."

Significant instances of corrupting parental influences also appear in *David Copperfield,* where, together with the treatment of the surrogate parent (discussed in chapter 5), they constitute an additional pattern controlling the organization of this novel. Here one parent who must reap as she has sown is the mother of James Steerforth. So doting is she that she seems unable to think or speak of any subject but her son. A strand of his baby hair is enclosed in her locket; his current portrait is always worn at her breast; all his letters are kept in a cabinet by her fireside chair. "A little vain and prosy about me," he calls her, "but that you can forgive her." And so we might. But in her idolatry she is blind to his faults as she is to her own, those very qualities which he has absorbed from her example. Mrs. Steerforth is proud, imperious, strongwilled, and unbending beneath any authority, insensitive to the feelings of those in inferior positions—as evidenced in her relationship with her ward and companion, the apologetic Rosa Dartle. That until James is grown no conflict develops between two such unyielding natures is due to the mother's complete indulgence of the son's desires, her staunch support of what she terms his "high spirit." It is this spirit, she explains, which caused her to send him to Salem House, a lesser school, where the headmaster would recognize his superiority and bow to it. This, she was satisfied, had aided her son's development, for free from constraint as the acknowledged "monarch of the place . . . he haughtily determined to be worthy of his station" (Chap. 20).

But it is precisely his belief in his own "superiority" that makes Steerforth insensitive to the feelings of others. An early instance occurs at Salem House when he confronts one of the masters, Mr. Mell, who has just ordered a roomful of noisy boys to be silent. Defiantly Steerforth responds with "silence yourself" and, when rebuked as the chief troublemaker in abetting the younger boys, retaliates by calling Mr. Mell "an impudent beggar," an intolerable insult to the underpaid, shabbily dressed man whose mother lives in an almshouse. Later, when rebuked by another pupil for hurting Mr. Mell's feelings, Steerforth exclaims disdainfully, "His feelings! His feelings will soon get the better of it, I'll be bound. His feelings are not like yours . . ." (Chap. 7).

Such arrogant insensitivity he displays again when he prepares for his first visit to the Yarmouth home of Mr. Peggotty. "Why, there's a pretty wide separation between them and us," he remarks coolly. "They are not to be expected to be as sensitive as we are. Their delicacy is not to be shocked, or hurt very easily. They are wonderfully virtuous, I dare say, . . . and they may be thankful that, like their coarse rough skins, they are not easily wounded" (Chap. 20).

This prejudicial view of class structure helps to explain why Steerforth repays the hospitality of the Peggottys by ruthlessly destroying their happiness. Cool, calculating, self-serving, he leads Emily to believe that he will make a lady of her, then abandons her after the thrill of conquest has passed. (At the same time one must remember that Emily, too, in the view then current, is at fault, for she hopes to rise out of her class. In the Victorian novel such ambition is usually disastrous.) Through his behavior Steerforth has also hurt the proud mother who shaped his character. Now she can only complain bitterly that her son, the "object" of her life, from whom she has had "no separate existence since his birth," has repaid her confidence with "systematic deception." Yet even in her grief she remains imperious. Vowing that her son shall never come near her, living or dead, unless he comes "humbly" and begs "forgiveness," she insists that "this is the acknowledgment I *will have.*" After listening to this bitter speech, David reflects: "While I heard and saw the mother as she said these words, I seemed to hear and see the son, defying them. All that I had ever seen in him in an unyielding, willful spirit, I saw in her" (Chap. 32).

Despite his uncommon abilities and, on occasion, engaging manners, Steerforth wastes his talents, all because he is the "heir of [his mother's] bringing-up." Even he feels at times that, properly disciplined and directed, he could have been a better person. "I wish to God I had had a judicious father these last twenty years!" he exclaims after tormenting himself during one of his rare twinges of conscience. "I wish with all my soul I had been better guided! . . . I wish with all my soul I could guide myself better!" (Chap. 22).

Because Steerforth has brought tragedy to two simple, decent men who depend upon the sea for their livelihood, he must atone during a violent storm, when the sea has its revenge. It is poetically just that his undisciplined life should end in drowning off the Yarmouth coast and that he should be washed up "among the ruins of the home he had wronged" (Chap. 55). When David delivers the crushing news to Mrs. Steerforth, she, like Anthony Chuzzlewit, reaps the harvest of her seeding. In this instance, however, it is not only her anguished cries but also the outbursts of Rosa Dartle that highlight the garnering. "Now," rages Rosa, who can conceal her mad and jealous love for Steerforth no longer, "is your pride appeased, you madwoman?" Calling her a "proud mother of a proud false son," she shows no mercy. "Moan for your nurture of him, moan for your loss of him! . . . You, who from his cradle reared him to be what he was, and stunted what he should have been!" (Chap. 56).

This scene sets the stage for the decline of the once formidable woman. Unable to endure the loss of one she considered inseparable from herself, smitten at last by a realization of her responsibility for his ruin, she escapes into the "querulous, imbecilic, fearful wandering" of senility, from which at times sudden reminders

Fig. 19. "I am the bearer of sad tidings," illustration by Hablôt K. Browne (Phiz) from *David Copperfield*

rouse her to relive the agonizing hour that brought her word of her son's death.

Equally culpable in the ruin of her son is Mrs. Heep in *David Copperfield*. Although the object of her idolatry lacks the surface attractions of Mrs. Steerforth's son (Uriah is cursed with a moist "skeleton hand" and lashless eyes like "two red suns" in a "cadaverous face"), the end product of both mother-son pairs is the same: each is concerned solely with himself, destroys the happiness of others, and ultimately suffers the consequences, whose impact also involves the mother.

The insistence of the Heeps on false humility notwithstanding ("umble we are, umble we have been, umble we shall ever be"), their inflated self-esteem makes them insensitive to others as does the Steerforths' arrogant pride. Even worse, it nurtures a rapacity that plunders all who, however decent and well-intentioned, stand in its way. Through his choice of two families, socially poles apart, Dickens shows that overweening maternal ambition is not peculiar to a particular class.

Uriah's crafty self-promotion under the guise of humility, his fawning self-effacement to find favor with his superiors, his stealthy usurpation of Mr. Wickfield's business, his outright theft of Aunt Betsey's deed, and his pleasure in tormenting Dr. Strong by divulging a domestic secret—all are traceable to his upbringing. Like Mrs. Steerforth Mrs. Heep dotes on her son and declares that all she wants from life is to see him "well settled." To achieve this end she has taught him to pounce upon unsuspecting victims and wring them dry for information of possible usefulness. Such a victim, David recalls, he himself was on his first visit to the Heep home. "The skill with which the one followed up whatever the other said" displayed a "touch of art" that he as a young boy was not proof against. Like a pair of "corkscrews" working on a "tender cork" they "wormed" information out of him that he had "no desire to tell" (Chap. 17). On a later visit David likens mother and son to "two great bats hanging over the whole house" (Chap. 39).

When at last Uriah is unmasked and his crimes come to light, Mrs. Heep resorts to the old strategy of feigning humility. "Ury, Ury!" she pleads, "be umble and make terms. I know my son will be umble, gentlemen, if you'll give him time to think" (Chap. 52).

But Uriah orders her to hold her noise (she has insisted that she will be "umble" for him) and tells her to get the stolen deed. Here mother and son, who until now have maintained a closely knit partnership, experience a breach initiated by the son, as it was with the Steerforths. Uriah ignores his mother's entreaties, just as Steerforth disregarded his mother's social bias when he eloped with Emily. Both sons finally pay for their wrongs: Steerforth with his life, Uriah with imprisonment.

It may have been personal pique that led Dickens, perhaps unconsciously, to choose the most autobiographical of his novels to present two such condemnatory portraits of mothers who fail their sons. Though in *The Battle of Life* (1846) he had honored the "Great character of mother, that . . . purifies the heart," it obviously was a sentiment that he had difficulty in applying to his own mother.

Unlike the novels so far considered in this chapter, *Hard Times* makes the parent-child relationship function organically to reinforce its primary purpose: to attack nineteenth-century philosophical radicalism. Rather than a realistic treatment of family conflicts, it is a devastating comment on the absurdity of a utilitarian system that ignores human values and calculates results in statistical averages. This shift in emphasis does not, however, make less explicit the theme of parental responsibility for the failings of the misguided child. In spite of what Ruskin called its "color of caricature," within its parabolic framework *Hard Times*, like *Martin Chuzzlewit* and *David Copperfield*, demonstrates that a parent must reap as he sows. In support of this thesis the three parts are appropriately entitled "Sowing," "Reaping," and "Garnering."

With his educational system of hard facts Gradgrind dehumanizes life as he molds his children by an impoverished curriculum that inhibits imagination, stultifies independent thought, and devalues the arts: "No little Gradgrind had ever seen a face in the moon. . . . No little Gradgrind had ever learnt the silly jingle, Twinkle, twinkle, little star; how I wonder what you are! No little Gradgrind had ever known wonder on the subject, each little Gradgrind having at five years old dissected the Great Bear like a Professor Owen, and driven Charles's Wain like a locomotive engine-driver" (I, 3). In the Gradgrind system there is no room for fancy, no time for wonder; all must give way to hard facts and "gloomy statistics." This strictly utilitarian and mechanistic diet inevitably starved the spirit of Louisa Gradgrind. "You have been so careful of me," she tells her father as she approaches a loveless marriage with apathetic detachment, "that I have never had a child's heart" (I, 15).

Constantly "grinding at the mill of knowledge," Louisa has grown tired, has, in fact, been tired a long time. Indifferent after an emotionally debilitating childhood, she offers no resistance to an arranged marriage with Bounderby, that predatory industrialist who acquires her as just another of his assets. Later, when she is almost lured into an adulterous relationship with the philandering James Harthouse, there appears to be little in "her soul for [him] to destroy. . ." (II, 7). (The would-be seducer, significantly, is also the end product of his early upbringing. Overindulged by parents, Harthouse is a man without purpose, motivated solely by self-interest.) Her ruin only narrowly averted, Louisa reproaches her father: "How could you give me life, and take from me all the inappreciable things that raise it from the state of conscious death? Where are the graces of my soul? Where are the sentiments of my heart? What have you done . . . with the garden that should have blossomed once, in this great wilderness here!" (II, 12). She pleads, "Save me by some other means!" and falls at his feet. With Louisa, "the triumph" of his "system," reduced to an "insensible heap," Gradgrind reaps in remorse the harvest of his sowing.

Whereas Louisa is the chief victim of the Gradgrind system, her brother Tom exploits it to become "that not unprecedented triumph of calculation which is usually at work on number one" (I, 9). He assesses everything in terms of personal advantage. Even the sisterly devotion of Louisa, all other outlets for affection having been denied her, he abuses to promote his selfish ends. Her miserable union with Bounderby he sees only as an access to ready cash. When she is unable finally to satisfy his increasing demands, he repays her love with angry ingratitude. Even after he robs a bank and is captured, Tom remains impenitent, so dehumanizing has been the Gradgrind system. Sullen and unmoved as he explains how his earlier embezzlement of funds made the bank robbery necessary, he responds without emotion to his father's shocked reaction: "I don't see why. So many people, out of so many, will be dishonest. I have ever heard you talk, a hundred times, of its being a law. How can *I* help laws? You have comforted others in such things, father. Comfort yourself!" (III, 7). Having heard Tom carry the principle of statistical averages to its logical conclusion, Gradgrind has to accept the failure of his system in this unfeeling "heir of [his] bringing-up."

However dehumanizing his mechanical system, Gradgrind is not an irredeemably bad man. Despite his seeming lack of feeling, he does have a heart, as is shown when he offers Sissy Jupe refuge after her father's disappearance. And he is deeply troubled when he sees how his educational philosophy has all but destroyed his children. In a way he reaps a second harvest. Unlike the first, a near-tragedy, the second restores human values. By taking Sissy into his home, Gradgrind had planted the seeds of love. It is this love which rescues Louisa for a measure of future contentment, enables Tom to escape to a new life and find repentance, and shows Gradgrind how to make "his facts and figures subservient to Faith, Hope, and Charity" (III, 9).

In the decade covered by the foregoing three novels there is a marked advance in artistry as Dickens concentrates on the thesis that the delinquent parent must ultimately pay for perverting the child's character. In *Martin Chuzzlewit* the remorseful father exclaims, "This crime began with me," a bare statement of the obvious, without the complex soul-searching which might have sharpened the emotional impact. With *David Copperfield* the method is more effective. Mrs. Steerforth, still unaroused to her own guilt, is humbled and made aware by an outside agent, Rosa. Yet the most successfully orchestrated humbling of the parent occurs in *Hard Times*. It is the victims themselves, his own children, who force Gradgrind to recognize the failure of his educational system. As the products of the hard-facts school that forbade flights of fancy and denied them their childhood, in a time of crisis they can only turn on him. "I curse the hour in which I was born to such destiny," cries Louisa before she confesses her near flight with Harthouse (II, 12). And Tom, told that he must go abroad to avoid prosecution, further condemns his upbringing. "I can't be more miserable anywhere," he whimpers, "than I have been here, ever since I can remember" (III, 7).

Added to the accusations of his own children are the devastating comments of the cool and calculating Bitzer, the most successful product of the Gradgrind system. Motivated solely by self-interest, Bitzer expects to fill Tom's place at the bank as a reward for delivering him to the authorities. Against Gradgrind's plea for mercy, for some sign of gratitude for his education, Bitzer stands firm. "I really wonder," he argues, in terms learned in Gradgrind's school, "to find you taking a position so untenable. My schooling was paid for; it was a bargain; and when I came away, the bargain ended" (III, 8). Admitting that his education was cheap, he climaxes his remarks by spouting a salient principle of his indoctrination: "I was made in the cheapest market, and have to dispose myself in the dearest" (III, 8). So, with his children and star pupil supplying the evidence, Gradgrind sees himself convicted. The impact of his crushing failure is far greater than Anthony Chuzzlewit's simple admission of guilt or Mrs. Steerforth's cowering submission before Rosa Dartle.

Two further instances of flawed parental guidance deserve mention. In *Great Expectations* Startop has been spoiled by an overprotective mother. Kept at home when he should have been at school, he has become "devotedly attached to her" and admires her "beyond measure." Denied an opportunity to develop manliness, he has "a woman's delicacy of features . . . exactly like" hers (Chap. 25). Because of his mother fixation he is ill prepared to cope with a man's world. With Eugene Wrayburn in *Our Mutual Friend* it is a domineering father who has weakened the son by choosing for him a career and role in life. As Eugene tells it, it was "pre-arranged for myself that I was to be the barrister I am (with the slight addition of an enormous practice which has not accrued), and also the married man I am not" (I, 12). Having decided nothing for himself, he feels no commitment to his law career. He pursues it with lassitude and accepts undistinguished results with apathetic resignation. Only after Lizzie Hexam enters his life does it take on meaning.

As Dickens saw it, parents generally were either too selfish or too preoccupied to give priority to the building of their children's character. The examples cited here show fathers who are blatantly covetous like Anthony Chuzzlewit or, like Gradgrind, devoid of human understanding and imagination. In their cold calculations they represent a society where money and statistics replace feelings. As for the mothers, their pride in their sons is actually self-centered. Mrs. Steerforth sees hers as a superior extension of herself. Through such pride she brings about his ruin and seals her own fate as well. Mrs. Heep, despite her pretended humility, is likewise guilty of a corrupting pride as she supports her unscrupulous Uriah in his predatory designs. That in every instance the perversion of the children recoils upon the parents shows how sternly Dickens viewed their guilt. To carry the argument a step further, since Dickens felt that a nation's leaders must, like parents, promote the moral well-being of their constituents, he obviously held them responsible for the rampant social corruption in nineteenth-century England. It follows, then, that, like parents, they also deserved to be punished.

Chapter 8

"The Dire Reversal of . . . Parent and Child"

"The whole idecorous threadbare ruin . . . grovelled. Not with any sense worthy to be called a sense, of this dire reversal of the places of parent and child, but in a pitiful expostulation to be let off from a scolding."

Our Mutual Friend (II, 2)

Among the multitude of parent-child portraits in Dickens's novels, one pattern—that in which parent and child exchange places—recurs so constantly as to appear nothing less than an obsession. What led Dickens to harp so persistently on this one string? All those responsible, old-before-their-time, self-supporting young people: are they the exaggerated glorification of that twelve-year-old boy who earned his own bread for a few months in a London warehouse? Are they a reflection of filial vexations lingering in their creator's adult life?

As early as *Nicholas Nickleby* (1838–39) Dickens's fictional parents are portrayed as selfishly manipulating their children into the unnatural role of provider and burden bearer. The most reprehensible of these is Walter Bray, a bankrupt living in the Rules of the King's Bench Prison, a man of "violent and brutal temper." Having ruined himself financially and physically through dissolute wastefulness, he now depends solely on Madeline, his motherless daughter, to provide him with his creature comforts through the sale of her small drawings and ornamental objects. To satisfy his selfish demands, she uncomplainingly slaves long hours over her pitifully paid art commissions. Even Vincent Crummles, who, unlike Bray, manifests a certain affection for his daughter, is not above fitting her into his self-serving

119

scheme. So that audiences will be impressed by her precosity in playing mature roles, she "has been kept up late every night, and put upon an unlimited allowance of gin-and-water from infancy, to prevent her growing tall . . ." (Chap. 23). Finally, there is the addlepated Mrs. Nickleby, who, with visions of being initiated into high society, is willing to sacrifice her daughter, Kate, to the dissipated Sir Mulberry Hawk.

In another early novel, *The Old Curiosity Shop* (1840–41), Dickens uses a grandfather and his granddaughter to illustrate the parent-child inversion. Little Nell, abnormally wise and devoted for her years, not only assumes the old man's duties, but also tries to save him from his mania for gambling. As he declines mentally and morally he becomes, in Dickens's words, "a mere child—a poor thoughtless, vacant creature" (I, 29). The normal roles of adult and child are further reversed as Nelly guides her grandfather in their wanderings across the countryside and provides his food and shelter with her meager earnings. "My grey-haired child has only me to help him," she explains (I, 31). Sitting by his bed as he drops off to sleep, she plans and prays for him. Like a loving mother she forgives him when he steals and gambles away her savings for their future, and removes him from temptation when she suspects him of planning a robbery. Before her health finally breaks she manages to place him in a haven where friends will look after him. With her mission accomplished, she dies, a fictional event that "jar[red] two hemispheres"—to borrow a phrase from Thomas Hardy.

From the host of parent-child inversions pervading Dickens's mature work, where careful plans conform to a central design, this chapter will choose examples that highlight the following novels: *Dombey and Son* (1846–48), *David Copperfield* (1849–50), *Bleak House* (1852–53), *Little Dorrit* (1855–57), and *Our Mutual Friend* (1864–65).

In *Dombey and Son* two mother-daughter situations from mutually exclusive circles parallel each other. Although they represent vastly different cultural backgrounds, the two pairs repeat each other to demonstrate their universal sisterhood. Just as the derelict Good Mrs. Brown once exploited the physical attractions of her daughter, Alice Marwood, so Mrs. Skewton has virtually sold her daughter, Edith Granger, by pushing her into a loveless marriage with Dombey. In each situation there is a reversal of roles: the daughter, smitten with remorse, turns on her mother, who becomes the chastised child.

When Alice Marwood, hard and bitter, returns after being transported, she rebukes her mother: "I don't know who began to harden me, if my own dear mother didn't." Recalling her neglected childhood, through which she somehow preserved her good looks ("so much the worse," she adds), she charges that she was "taught all wrong" (Chap. 34). Now hopeless and outcast, she sits in judgment on the one who must assume full responsibility for this tragedy. "Were this miserable mother, and this miserable daughter, only the reduction to their lowest grade, of certain social vices somehow prevailing higher up?" asks Dickens. "In this round world of many circles within circles, do we make a weary journey from the high grade to the low, to find at last . . . that the two extremes touch, and that our Journey's end is but our starting place? Allowing for great difference of stuff and texture, was the pattern of this woof repeated among gentle blood at all?" (Chap. 24).

Answers to these questions are found in the relationship between Mrs. Skewton and Edith, representatives of the "gentle blood." Realizing that she will be selling herself like the lowest woman of the streets when she marries Dombey for his wealth and position, Edith rebukes her mother: "You know he has bought me. . . . God, that I have lived for this, and that I feel it!" What childhood, she asks, has she ever had? Her mother early made her a woman—"artful, designing, mercenary." She was taught to lay "snares for men" before she even understood the "base and wretched aim of every new display." Charging that she has never known "what it is to have an honest heart, and love," she recalls ruefully how she has been "hawked and vended" in English resorts until she has lost all self-respect and loathes herself (Chap. 27). All this so that her mother could share her daughter's wealth and station!

In a later confrontation, when Edith insists on shielding the innocent Florence from the malign influence of Mrs. Skewton, that vain, selfish woman can only wail childishly about duty towards parents in these "evil days." Edith concludes the scene with the resigned air of a mother who must make allowances for a child's irresponsible outbursts: "The object of our lives is won. Henceforth let us wear it silently. . . . I forgive your part in tomorrow's wickedness [her marriage to Dombey]. May God forgive my own!" (Chap. 30). Thereafter it is Edith who must exert a mother's control and care over the woman who once manipulated her but is soon reduced to the state of babbling infancy by the stroke that will bring her erring life to its close. This exchange of places between mother and daughter, like that of Good Mrs. Brown and Alice, is not only an illustration of family inversion, but a compelling argument that one moral law governs the whole human family regardless of differences in station.

In *David Copperfield* the relationship between Annie Strong and her mother, Mrs. Markleham (the "Old Soldier") is similar to that of Edith and Mrs. Skewton. A widow whose limited means will not support her in idleness or satisfy her craving for amusement, she exploits her daughter's marriage as a financial "boon." So long as she can spend two leisurely hours in the most comfortable chair reading her paper, and attend operas, concerts, and exhibitions, she is unconcerned over having matched her daughter with a man more than old enough to be her father. Unlike Edith Dombey, however, Annie Strong loves and respects her husband. And though her reproof does unmask her mother's self-serving and unconscionable manipulation, it is couched in more respectful and milder terms: "I never thought of any worldly gain that my husband would bring to me. . . . it was *you* who first presented to my mind the thought that any one could wrong me, and wrong him, by such cruel suspicion" (Chap. 45). Thus Mrs. Markleham is instructed by her own daughter. Chastened, she must henceforth respect as true marriage the union she once designed only as an arrangement of convenience to herself.

A different type of inversion is the relationship between Agnes Wickfield and her father, where the parent does not deliberately exploit the child, but becomes so dependent on her that she voluntarily makes his happiness the "utmost height" of her hope. By assuming full responsibility for their future, by devoting her life to him, she wants to repay him for the love and care he gave her in infancy after the death of her mother (Chap. 54). Because he has "narrowed the circle of his sympathies and duties, in the concentration of his whole mind" on her (Chap. 25), she considers herself the "innocent cause of his errors" (Chap. 26) when his weakness for drink makes him an easy prey to the slippery Uriah Heep, to whom he eventually loses the control of his business. With her father's increasing dependence on her, Agnes has become a mother figure. She always sits with him when he dines, watches for his despondent moods, and kisses him goodnight at bedtime. David doubts whether Wickfield could have dined without her: the food would have lacked its usual flavor if she had not served it (Chap. 15).

Their roles completely reversed, Agnes is the solicitous mother, Wickfield the sheltered son. When they sit by the fireside after dinner, she doles out his wine and he takes it "like a child." As he lies down on the sofa, she pillows his head (Chap. 35). But Wickfield admits that she has also filled the void left by his wife's untimely death: "My love for my dear child was a diseased love, but my mind was all unhealthy then" (Chap. 60). Here, then, is another dimension to the inversion pattern: the daughter as a wife-mother substitute. In his psychological penetration Dickens anticipated theories of the human psyche that were not to be articulated until after his time.

When with his next novel, *Bleak House*, Dickens began to focus on parental delinquencies as symptoms of a disordered society, he had become increasingly disillusioned about economic man, finding him parasitic, ruthless, predatory. Recurring instances of parent-child reversals witness to this disillusionment, especially those in which the parent is totally oblivious of the family's needs. A case in point is Mrs. Jellyby, who shirks all home responsibilities while organizing a mission to the natives of Borrioboola-Gha. Always "seeming to look a long way off," as if she can "see nothing nearer than Africa," she ignores her dirty children, who tumble about, notching "memoranda of their accidents on their legs" (Chap. 4). Her neglected husband is unhappy, and the unsupervised servants do what they like with the supplies, which the tradesmen deliver without any reference to need. Even during meals she dictates countless letters to her eldest daughter, Caddy, who is frustrated by lack of time to be a substitute mother to the family. For all her charitable interest in distant Africa, Mrs. Jellyby takes no notice of social needs nearer home. Of London's malodorous slums she seems unaware, even as the inhabitants breed disease that cannot be confined. The miseries of such vagrant orphans as Jo the crossing sweeper leave her unmoved.

Unlike the Jellyby household, where parental "telescopic philanthropy" has involved the neglected children in responsibilities beyond their years, the ménage of Harold Skimpole deteriorates under his parasitical idleness. With his specious arguments about the luxury of generosity (Chap. 6), the nonpayment of debts, and the meaning of time and money (Chap. 15), he is a sham, a parent infinitely more childlike than his own children, whom he lets shift for themselves as he flits about like a butterfly ("butterflies are free," Chap. 6). He has never looked after his children, explains Jarndyce, because he "wanted somebody to look after *him*. He is a child, you know!" (Chap. 6). And Skimpole himself admits that he has never grown up. Although Dickens himself could see the world with the eyes of a child and enter heartily into childhood fancy and play, he could not condone the adult irresponsibility which excluded serious endeavor in the grown-up world.

Another parasite is Turveydrop, whose very name suggests excrement. Exploiting his son by having him earn their living by conducting all the lessons in their dancing academy, he only stands before the fire, lounges in sartorial splendor at resorts, and dines in French restaurants. Meanwhile his shabbily dressed and poorly educated son works long hours and lunches on cold mutton. A "model of Deportment," as he wants to be known, Turveydrop has "everything but nature": a false complexion, false teeth, false whiskers, and a wig (Chap. 14). In short, he is nothing, or, like excrement, even worse.

With the introduction of Charley (Charlotte) Neckett, Dickens portrays a type of inversion in which it is society rather than an individual which has withdrawn from personal responsibility. Why should a girl of thirteen years take on a woman's work in supporting two younger children? With mother and father both dead, Charley tries to keep the little family together with sixpences and shillings from cleaning and washing. Even so, had not a kind landlady forgiven the rent on their chilly room, they would have had to move on. Jarndyce responds to this humanitarian gesture with a biblical echo: "forasmuch as she did it unto the least of these—!" (Chap. 15). But all too often, he implies, the world's orphans cannot turn to society for parental love.

As *Bleak House* moves from one unsatisfactory household to another, its variations of the inversion pattern illustrate the whole muddle of society as symbolized by the compelling fog metaphor in the opening chapter. The exploited children are but the victims of an order born of indifference and selfishness. Mrs. Jellyby is analogous to those Victorians concerned with the "white man's burden." What are foreign missions, asks Dickens, but an evasion of immediate responsibilities, if not even an exploitation of primitive people who would be happier left alone?

A different emphasis is intended with Skimpole. Perverting logical premises as he flippantly rationalizes his parasitic existence, he is a Carlylean Sir Jabesh Windbag or Viscount Mealymouth, guilty of "insolent Donothingism in Practice and Saynothingism in Speech" *(Past and Present,* III, ii). Even more despicable are men like Turveydrop, whose right to enjoy luxurious idleness is as false as everything about him, a leech thriving on the labors of his son.

Bleak House is one of Dickens's most persuasive arguments that abnormal family relationships invariably abound in a degenerate society. As Norman and Jeanne Mackenzie *(Dickens, a Life)* have pointed out, all its mysteries are a "riddle about parenthood, legitimacy, identity." Even Chancery itself is "a ghastly caricature of a family" and the Lord Chancellor "affords but a poor substitute for the love and pride of parents" (p. 255).

Little Dorrit documents further the interaction of the family and society. Again the focus is on the distorted parent-child relationship, sharpened this time by organic imagery. Because the principal characters are either confined to the Marshalsea or shackled by psychological fetters of their own forging, England is envisioned as one vast prison whose inmates are a hopelessly warped family. The theme of parent-child inversion emerges through the sacrificial devotion of the heroine, Amy, to her father, William Dorrit. Born in debtors' prison, where Dorrit has been detained for twenty-five years, Amy (Little Dorrit) would seem the least suited to assume the burdens thrust upon her. Yet she is the one practical member of the family: she finds employment for her shiftless brother, arranges dancing lessons and paid performances for her arrogant sister, and as a seamstress earns enough to provide her father with creature comforts.

William Dorrit, another parasite, preens himself as the Father of the Marshalsea; yet ironically he exercises no more paternal function toward his fellow prisoners than toward his children, two of whom he has corrupted by his pretensions of gentility. He shamelessly allows Amy to assume the role of little mother to him and his other children, all the while keeping up the pretense that he is unaware of her going out to work. Like a spoiled child he is concerned only with his personal gratification. Never does he note that Amy's dress is shabby, that her shoes are worn, or that she goes to bed supperless so that he may have her portion of meat. Quite unabashedly he even suggests to Amy that she encourage young John Chivery's amorous attentions, so that he may receive special consideration from John's father, the prison turnkey. Amy tactfully gets him to see how base this suggestion is. Humiliated and ashamed, maudlin tears of self-pity flowing unchecked, he whines as he pushes away the plate she has set before him: "What does it matter whether I eat or starve?" (I, 19).

Like an indulgent mother, Amy, whose very name means "love," has mixed emotions as she recognizes her father's failings. Half-ashamed, yet proud and admiring, she is all-affectionate and protective. Aware of the false pride that will not let him admit that his children work for money, she tactfully invents various fictions to explain her daily absence.

When in true melodramatic style her father inherits a fortune and is released from prison, Little Dorrit happily anticipates the restoration of family dignity. "I shall see him, as I never saw him yet," she exults. "I shall see my dear love, with the dark cloud cleared away" (I, 35). But the cloud of selfishness and false dignity does not lift; and Dorrit, holding state in a luxurious Roman villa, no longer needs his daughter's ministrations. Her occupation gone, she can only sit back in her corner of their stately carriage, her hands folded, like a little mother whose work is done.

Even in his opulent new circumstances Dorrit indulges in self-pity, calling himself, with unconscious insight, a "poor wretch in

Fig. 20.   An Unexpected After-Dinner Speech, illustration by Hablôt
K. Browne (Phiz) from *Little Dorrit*

the midst of his wealth" (II, 5). Again, returning from a brief visit in London, and letting it be known that he has thus proved his independence of Amy, he is so inconsiderate as to accuse her of neglect (II, 19). Shortly thereafter, when he collapses at a public dinner, his mind reverts to the prison days from which he never really escaped. Pale and frightened, but not ashamed of being presented as one born and bred in prison, Little Dorrit rises to resume her earlier role of tender protectress. For ten days she watches over her sinking father until at last she sees his face gradually subside into a a younger likeness of her own (II, 19). At his death his youthful features reveal what he has always been: an erring child, loved and tenderly cared for by the motherly Amy. It is a deft touch to clinch this inverted relationship.

Amy figures in yet another adult-child reversal as she keeps a watchful eye on the retarded Maggie. A clumsy woman of twenty-eight, this simple creature looks to Amy for guidance and companionship while supporting herself by running errands. Mentally she will never be older than ten, at which age a fever arrested her development. The two make an incongruous couple, "the little mother attended by her big child" (I, 9); beside the large-boned Maggie Little Dorrit looks even slighter than usual. Here, as with Mr. Dick in *David Copperfield,* Dickens's portrayal of mental retardation reflects accurate observation.

For *Our Mutual Friend,* his last completed novel, Dickens reserved his darkest vision of the warped family and warped society. In the murky waters of the polluted Thames two unscrupulous and degraded men, Gaffer Hexam and Rogue Riderhood, fathers both, make their living as scavengers. That in a river awash with commercial and human wastes they plunder the victims of accident, suicide, and murder is symbolic of a sordid and acquisitive economy.

Both Hexam and Riderhood are unfit to be the fathers of the daughters who defend and care for them. Lizzie Hexam acts as a moral stay for her father, "keeping him as straight as [she] can," she tells her brother, "and hoping [she] may turn him to wish to do better things." Feeling thus responsible for her father, she refuses a tempting chance to leave him and better herself by education. "I must not think of it," she says. "The harder father is borne upon, the more he needs me to lean on." At the same time she arranges secretly for the education of her brother, thus trying to steer him away from his father's occupation and into a new life. And she admonishes him: "Be sure you always give your father his full due. . . . And if you should ever happen to hear anything said against your father that is new to you, it will not be true" (I, 6). With these words she resembles a loyal mother illogically defending a child whom she knows to be guilty.

More unfortunate than Lizzie, Pleasant Riderhood is the daughter of an actively cruel father, a man beyond redemption. There are even rumors that he sometimes kills the men he dredges from the river. Yet in spite of the brutal beatings he inflicts upon Pleasant, she supports him with her earnings from her pawnbroker's shop. And she mourns as for a wayward child when her father is dragged from the Thames, supposedly drowned. Then ensues a significant scene in which Riderhood, who has preyed on the dead and whose heart has long been as cold and empty as death, is "instinctively unwilling" to be revived back into the alien world of life; he "would be left dormant, if he could" (III, 3). As he regains consciousness Pleasant can only hope that all his evil has been drained away into the muddy waters and that only the good toward which she has tried to steer him will remain. It is, of course, a vain hope.

Another unredeemed parent in *Our Mutual Friend* is the father of Jenny Wren (Fanny Cleaver), the dolls' dressmaker, the shrewdest and probably the littlest of a train of young heroines whom Dickens sentimentalizes by the epithet "little." Something between a dwarf and a child, yet with a sharpness capable of penetrating any deception, Jenny has been surrounded by drunkenness from her cradle, has endured physical deformity and pain, and has struggled to support herself and her father. Her hardships have made her waspish, shrewish. Although her father is not actively wicked like Riderhood, he is, nonetheless, hopelessly derelict. A drunkard, always sponging off his daughter to quench his thirst, he is in constant disgrace. Jenny, refreshingly less meek in her devotion than Amy Dorrit, but no less genuine, calls him her "troublesome child," her "prodigal son" (II, 1). She tries to reform him by repeated tongue-lashings; she orders him not to leave the house in her absence; she threatens to desert him or have him picked up by the police to be jailed or transported—all in vain. "He's enough to break his mother's heart...," she laments. "I wish I had never brought him up." Although this "prodigal" always promises to reform, he daily sinks deeper into alcoholic stupor. "If he has no consideration for his liver," frets Jenny, "has he none for his mother?" (III, 10). She maintains this grotesque maternal stance even after his death in drunken delirium. "If my poor boy had been brought up better," she reflects, "he might have done better.... I couldn't always keep him near me. He got fractious and nervous, and I was obliged to let him go into the streets. And he never did well in the streets, he never did well out of sight. How often it happens to children!" She rues her past impatience: "If I had been patient, I should never have called him names. But I hope I did it for his good.... I was bound to try everything, you know, with such a charge on my hands" (IV, 8).

To portray a daughter's sacrificial dedication to a flawed father seems to have been an obsession with Dickens. As previously pointed out, such a relationship had already figured briefly in the earlier *Nicholas Nickleby*, where Madeline tirelessly supports the ill-tempered old Bray. A similar situation, treated incidentally in *Great Expectations*, involves Herbert Pocket's intended, Clara, and her father, Barley. Considerably abbreviated because it is not a central strand, it nevertheless repeats the pattern of the demanding father, confined to his room as an invalid, roaring for his grog, beating on the floor boards until the rafters threaten to collapse and feasting on mutton chops, potatoes, split peas, and double Gloucester while his daughter makes do with bread and cheese. Although minor characters, Madeline and Clara deserve to be mentioned as members of that gallery of daughters whose lives revolve around their fathers.

In the "dire reversal of the places of parent and child" is seen Dickens's recurring theme: a child's dedicated efforts to redeem a flawed parent through love. (That the effort succeeds only seldom, as with Florence Dombey and her father, may imply the advanced selfishness of the parent rather than any lack of potency in the remedy.) Having become increasingly pessimistic over the political structure of Victorian England and having given vent to his indignation in slashing attacks on the party system, Parliament, and governmental bureaucracy, Dickens gave force to his criticism through his unforgettable parent-child inversions. On a larger scale, these inversions function as unifying metaphors to carry his total vision of English society. Just as family after family is portrayed with the natural guardian assuming no control, so Victorian England is to be viewed as one vast family with indifferent and incompetent leadership. In short, the defaulting parent and the neglected child are to be recognized as the domestic equivalents of the bungling statesmen and their deserted constituents. That this darkening vision continued to oppress Dickens is borne out by his closing words in an address at the Birmingham and Midland Institute on 25 September 1869: "My faith in the people governing, is, on the whole, infinitesimal; my faith in The People governed, is, on the whole, illimitable."

Chapter 9

"Give Us ... Better Homes"

"Give us, in mercy, better homes when we're a-lying in our cradles."
The Chimes, Third Quarter

Viewing nineteenth-century society as disordered, and convinced that a host of defective parents and violated children were its inevitable result, Dickens saw contemporary family relationships as rarely harmonious. Consequently, few ideal families appear in his fiction. When they do they are usually minor characters and from the poorer classes—the Cratchits, the Vecks, the Toodles. More often Dickens saw the relationship between parent and child as an unhappy one, especially when they belong to the same sex.

With his own boyhood as background, Dickens found little to support the delineation of an ideal father-son rapport. There is, to be sure, the striking exception of Tony and Sam Weller in *Pickwick Papers.* This being Dickens's first novel, his early comradeship with his own father had not yet soured. His good-humored accounts of their relationship are not altogether unlike the jocular familiarity between the Wellers. Although Sam is well aware of Tony's faults (like John Dickens, he cannot be trusted with money), their relationship is one of camaraderie, an adult friendship with no burden of parental-filial obligation. Thus without disrespect Sam can address his father as "corpilence," "Old Codger,"and the like.

But, as Dickens found increasing reason for annoyance with his father's behavior, he seldom introduced a model father-son pair, at least not with his major characters. Actually, most of his heroes are fatherless. Where the plot includes a father with a grown son, good communication is usually absent (the Willets and the Chuzzlewits, for example, Jonas being the only son in

132

Dickens's novels to exceed the father in wickedness). There are, certainly, scattered instances of compatibility, but they are confined to fathers with young sons (like the Crunchers in *A Tale of Two Cities*) or minor characters, like Wemmick and his Aged P. in *Great Expectations*. Perhaps, as Eleanor Rooke has suggested, Dickens did not find enough enduring paternal instinct in himself to give life to the father-son theme in his books.[1]

Just as there is little communication between fathers and sons, so mothers generally do not enjoy a good relationship with grown daughters, especially when the father is still living. Usually the mothers are responsible for the friction. The ill-tempered Mrs. Varden *(BR)*, not content to inflict her snappishness on her husband, extends her abusiveness to their daughter, Dolly, probably because she is his favorite. Having selfishly exploited their daughters, both Mrs. Skewton and Good Mrs. Brown *(DS)* have set up barriers that produce estrangement and recrimination. Although the relationship between Annie Strong and her mother, Mrs. Markleham *(DC)*, endures less strain, it also suffers from the selfishness of an exploiting parent. Between Bella Wilfer and her mother *(OMF)* there is constant bickering, aggravated by the latter's discontent and self-pity.

Brighter portraits emerge from the mother-son relationships, which as a rule are not marred by cold indifference and explicit hostility. Usually the mother is affectionate, sometimes excessively, and protective. Notable examples are Mrs. Maylie and Harry *(OT);* Mrs. Nubbles and Kit *(OCS);* Mrs. Rudge and Barnaby, *(BR);* Polly Toodle and Bob the Grinder *(DS);* Clara Copperfield and David *(DC);* the Rouncewells and the Woodcourts *(BH);* and Mrs. Crisparkle and Septimus *(ED)*. Mrs. Rouncewell, inspired in part by recollections of Dickens's paternal grandmother, as pointed out earlier, is one of his truly noble mothers: she never loses faith in George, her prodigal son, and gives him her unquestioning love and understanding on his return, even though his absence has given her great anxiety. Unlike such admirable attachments are those where mothers, through indulgence, spoil or pervert their sons: Mrs. Leeford and Monks *(OT)*, the Steerforths and the Heeps *(DC)*, and Mrs. Merdle and Sparkler, as well as Mrs. Gowan and Harry *(LD)*. Given Dickens's long entrenched bitterness toward his own mother, the occasional satisfactory mother-son relationship in his novels may constitute a wish fulfillment. As already suggested in chapter 5, the early death of Clara Copperfield in the most autobiographical of his works may signify that his own mother was dead to Dickens when she killed his love and trust.

The closest family ties exist between Dickens's fathers and daughters. Featured in his early, middle, and late novels, such relationships seem to have fascinated him throughout his career. Typical is Vincent Crummles, who, though he exploits his daughter to promote his theatre, regards her with pride and affection *(NN)*. And Gabriel Varden is exceedingly fond of Dolly and lavishes her with attention *(BR)*. Pride and protectiveness motivate Mr. Spenlow as he shields his motherless Dora *(DC)*. The strongest ties bind Agnes Wickfield to her father, who needs her love and protection. The overworked Caddy Jellyby enjoys the understanding and sympathy of her father, inasmuch as both have suffered from Mrs. Jellyby's missionary zeal *(BH)*. And Dr. Manette returns to the world of reality through the devoted ministrations of his daughter, Lucie *(TTC)*. Mr. Meagles and Pet *(LD)*, Toby Veck and Meg *(The Chimes)* are other examples.

A different kind of father-daughter relationship exists between Bella Wilfer and her father, actually a type of reversal *(OMF)*. But here the inversion, instead of undergirding serious political criticism, is portrayed with playful mock-seriousness. "You are the best of all the dearest boys that ever were." Bella tells her father (IV, 4). And indeed, he is worthy of her praise, a rare specimen in Dickens's gallery of fathers who are mothered by their daughters. As if he were a schoolboy, Bella chides him for his grubby hands. She carves his meat, pours his drink. "We must keep his little clothes clean," she warns as she ties a napkin under his chin at dinner (IV, 5). In short, she makes a plaything of him. She also plans surreptitious meetings, as if they were carrying on a secret love affair. Yet if this mother-*cum*-lover behavior strikes the modern reader as ludicrous at times, or even repellent, that is obviously not the author's intention.

What underlies the recurrence of the mothering daughter in Dickens? Before he was mature enough to dispense with the usual tender maternal attentions in boyhood, the cord that bound him to his mother was rudely severed. Denied his birthright of normal pampering and petting, he forever after viewed maternal indulgence, whatever its guise, with an excess of sentimentality. The father of two grown daughters, both devoted, he may well have fancied receiving from them the sort of playful, indulgent, mock-maternal treatment which Bella Wilfer lavishes on her little pa. Like the possible wish fulfillment suggested earlier in connection with the mother-son portraits, such mothering would substitute for what he had lacked while growing up. (Ironically, though, no parent so dominant and self-sufficient as Dickens would be likely to inspire such teatment.) At any rate, he clearly expects us to be enchanted by Bella's attitude and to envy her father.

Obviously Dickens's fictional parents have a preference for a child of the opposite sex. Between fathers and sons, and mothers and daughters, there is often alienation marked by distrust and bitterness, especially when the relationship is inverted. Dickens's personal involvement in this relationship was apparently the inspiration for the portraits whose validity would later be confirmed by Freudian psychology.

Regardless of his preference for the father-daughter attachment, however, when Dickens champions the abandoned child it is the boys, not the girls, who are most abused, neglected, and lonely. (Little Nell is a notable exception.) None of his heroines are so completely rejected as Oliver Twist, David Copperfield, and Jo the crossing sweeper. Always it is the author's never-to-be-forgotten past that colors these portraits. Again it should be noted that the accounts of Oliver's and David's childhood miseries owe their poignancy to Dickens's rendering of his own boyhood and his gratitude to providence for preserving his better self from temptation and danger. For Jo's oppression the blame lies with society, where the delinquencies of individual parents merge into one vast delinquency. When such children are abandoned by their natural guardians and all others, then, as James Hannay, one of Dickens's *Household Words* contributors, observes, "the nursing-mother Britannia takes them to her bosom, imprisons, transports, and privately whips them, with the kindliest intentions; and at the same time the ghastliest feeling that it is not all right" ("Lambs to Be Fed," 30 August 1851).

Because Dickens believed, on the basis of his own experience and observation, that few parents enjoy a happy family relationship, some of his most appealing characters are childless. Yet, significantly, they may assume parental responsibilities as surrogates, as explained in chapter 5. When they do, they are model parents. As with Kipling later, most of Dickens's good parents are foster parents. Here, as mentioned earlier, belong some of his especially likable characters, the bachelors, as if actual fatherhood might pose too great a strain on their wholly laudable character: the Cheerybles *(NN)*, Riah and Tremlow *(OMF)*, and Crisparkle *(ED)* are cases in point.[2]

* * *

That Dickens kept returning to the theme of the delinquent parent and the homeless and alienated child in search of identity is evidence, as already submitted, that his own boyhood had left impressions never to be obliterated. His own past neglect became inseparable from the general character of the age. Prisons, impecunious fathers, exploitive mothers, violated and captive children, all of which keep recurring in his novels with increasing emphasis, he was to see as a microcosm of nineteenth-century England. When hundreds of little street Arabs must pillage and starve, when young factory workers were mangled by unfenced machinery or exhausted before their time, when minors were transported or hanged for misdemeanors, when, in brief, there was no escape for those doomed from infancy to crime or early death, then something was drastically wrong with society. "Let the reader go into the children's side of any prison in England," Dickens admonished the public in his preface to *Martin Chuzzlewit,* "or, I grieve to add, of many workhouses, and judge whether those are monsters who disgrace our streets, people our hulks and penitentiaries, and overcrowd our penal colonies, or are creatures whom we have deliberately suffered to be bred for misery and ruin."

His personal recollections fused with an awareness of childhood abuses all about him, Dickens lashed out at a political system that could tolerate such conditions. As early as 1839 he satirized slippery politicians in his portrait of Mr. Gregsbury, the M. P. of Manchester Buildings, Westminster *(NN)*. By 1852 he was attacking more fiercely, ridiculing the party system with its Coodle, Doodle, Foodle, Hoodle, Loodle, and Poodle—all apathetic

to the social outcasts in Tom-all-Alone's *(BH)*. In 1854 he casti-
gated Parliament, "that great cinder heap where Gradgrind sifts
the odds and ends he wants and throws the dust into the eyes of
other people who want other odds and ends" *(HT)*. Parliament,
he charged that same year, was full of "shocking mountebanks
. . . contesting for places, power, and patronage" ("To Working
Men," *HW*, 7 October 1854). In 1855 he branded governmental
red tape and incompetence as the Circumlocution Office *(LD)*.
With each successive novel his criticism grew more caustic, until it
reached its climax in a devastating picture of political maneuvering during Veneering's campaign, highlighted by vulgar dinners
and banal oratory *(OMF)*. Equally reprehensible here is the pon-
tificating Podsnap with his smug complacency, his overweening
pride in the British system, and his contempt for all things foreign. That Dickens kept this darkening vision of England to the
last is borne out by his satirical thrust in the unfinished *Edwin
Drood*, where Mr. Sapsea displays the national bias by blasting
everything "Un-English" and singing songs regretting the small-
ness of "a nation of hearts of oak" in comparison with "so many
verminous people" elsewhere (Chap. 12).

Having lost hope in the ballot because people would not help
themselves, Dickens was convinced that both the church and the
country faced ruin.[3] It should be noted, however, that he han-
dled his criticism on different levels. In his earlier novels evils are
objectified through specific villains: Fagin, Sikes, and Monks
(OT), Squeers and Ralph Nickleby *(NN)*, Quilp *(OCS)*, Rudge and
Chester *(BR)*, Jonas Chuzzlewit and Pecksniff *(MC)*. Here Dickens is a tireless crusader for the workhouse Olivers, the undernourished and oppressed boys in cheap boarding schools like Dotheboys Hall, the sexually attractive Little Nells menaced by the
lascivious oglings of lustful Quilps. In the later novels the emphasis shifts from portraits of individual villains to an attack on society and its institutions for engendering evils, with certain persons
manipulating the destructive forces and others becoming its victims. Here public attitudes toward children serve as an index to
what is wrong. Thus the young Florence Dombey's isolation and
rejection are directly traceable to her father's having become the
product of an age dominated by commerce and soulless calculation. This also explains Louisa Gradgrind's plight. In *Little Dorrit*,

moreover, Amy is an exploited child, not because her father is wicked, but because he himself is the victim of brutal social forces. And in *Great Expectations* Magwitch, cast off by society in childhood, seeks revenge by manipulating Pip to breach the social barriers as a gentleman. Parasitism in *Bleak House*, the ruthless suppression of emotion and fancy in *Hard Times*, the blind worship of status and the cloaking of guilt with false religion in *Little Dorrit*, outright hostility and blatant exploitation in *Our Mutual Friend*—all simultaneously victimize children and erode the state through social greed, selfishness, and indifference to human dignity.

That Dickens's most vehement indictments of nineteenth-century England coincided with his later discouragement over the affairs of his own family bears repeating. Compounding the brooding consciousness of a broken home, with his wife banished and a stranger to Gad's Hill except for secret visits,[4] were the failures of his sons and his guilt over the unsatisfactory marriage of his daughter Katey. In the belief that his name would be his children's "best possession,"[5] had Dickens perhaps overcompensated for his own unhappy boyhood? Had he been too determined to ensure their future security? Now that his sons' lack of perseverance and want of purpose in finding their groove had become all too apparent, did he experience doubts about his parental adequacy? To be sure, he had repeatedly attributed their lassitude to a weakness inherited from their mother. But as he acknowledged a share of the blame for the domestic rupture, might he not also have admitted its part (and therefore his own) in accounting for his sons' poor performance?

Whatever his gnawing doubts about his role as husband and father, as Dickens interpreted and transformed his personal experience, his darkening mood helped to shape his total vision of society. Viewing inadequate parents and their wronged children as symptomatic of a nation that has lost its values, he crusaded for a restoration of the home to its rightful place in building future generations. Only then could the stability of the state be assured. "Give us, in Mercy, better homes when we're a-lying in our cradles," Dickens pleaded in *The Chimes* (Third Quarter). Basic human rights would demand better food, better working conditions, a system of justice without the constant threat of punishment—in a word, love. (Whatever his shortcomings as a father, Dickens can certainly not be accused of failing to give his children his sincere affection, constant concern, and the material requirements of a good home. As previously stated, he was ahead of his time in organizing his household with their needs—physical, intellectual, and spiritual—in mind. That some of his practices were contrary to those recommended today is hardly a fair basis for criticism. Were he living now he would doubtless weigh and adopt different methods.)

Along with better homes and decent living conditions children were to enjoy untroubled years. "Rigour and cruelty in childhood," Dickens maintained, would inevitably violate their spirit and intellect. Instead of being treated as small adults mechanically digesting hard facts, being rushed through changes that should come about normally, children should be allowed to dream and wonder, to experience the full play of fancy, to develop creative imagination. For Dickens could always see how the world looked through the eyes of a child. "The dreams of childhood," he mused, "its airy fables; its graceful, beautiful, humane, impossible adornments of the world beyond: so good to be believed in once, so good to be remembered when outgrown" (*HT*, II, 9). Dickens had indeed taken the New Testament admonition to heart: "Except ye . . . become as little children, ye shall not enter into the Kingdom of Heaven." Thus it is well "not to be too wise, not to be too stately, not to be too rough with innocent fancies, or to treat them with too much lightness—. . . for this is the spirit inculcated by One on whose knees children sat. . . ."[6]

Nothing must hamper natural development or interfere with the right to be a child. "I had rather be a child," insists little Paul Dombey when Dr. Blimber proposes making a man of him (Chap. 11). "Nature wants children to be children before they are men," said Rousseau, a statement which Dickens emphatically supported. "If we deliberately prevent this order, we shall get premature fruits which are neither ripe nor well-flavored, and which soon decay. . . . Childhood has ways of seeing, thinking, and feeling peculiar to itself; nothing could be more foolish than to substitute our ways for them,"[7] as is the case with Ruth Pinch's pupil, "a premature little woman of thirteen years old, who had already arrived at such a pitch of whalebone and education that she had nothing girlish about her: which was a source of great rejoicing to all her relatives and friends" (*MC,* Chap. 9).

Not allowing a child to develop naturally by encouraging individual tastes and attitudes might well result in a warped adult, a case of prolonged immaturity like that of Abel Garland (*OCS*). Although the Garlands appear to be a closely knit family, Dickens sees their relationship as deplorable. Abel, who has never been separated from his parents except for weekends—and these always made him miserable—, models himself on his father by copying his dress (he has even inherited his father's clubfoot). Never permitted a will of his own, he has not cared to make decisions for himself. His absolute submission to his father has made him passive, purposeless, incapable of independent action. Only if a child is allowed to mature normally in accord with his natural bent, so Dickens implies, will he become an adult with an integrated personality, not a grown-up juvenile.

To enjoy a normal development, Dickens maintains, children must be treated as individuals, not things. Nothing so robs a human being of dignity as to depersonalize him. The chief fault of the Gradgrind educational system is that it treats the pupils as things, mechanically parroting facts by rote. The failure to recognize each child as a separate human being with individual capacities for enjoying life clearly parallels the cold indifference of the Coketown employers to the individual needs of their workers, referred to impersonally as "the Hands"—"a race who would have found more favour with some people," adds Dickens, "if Providence had seen fit to make them only hands or, like the lower creatures of the seashore, only hands and stomachs—" (*HT,* I, 10).

* * *

Because Dickens saw the home and family as the foundation of national well-being, the parent-child relationship was to be one of the most important and the longest sustained of his interests. It was to warn of national disaster that he portrayed the homelessness and misery to which thousands had been doomed from infancy. As he unflaggingly, obsessively, championed their cause, he focused on the principal victims: the orphans, the children of indifferent or cruel parents, the children corrupted by designing or misguided parents, and the children exploited to assume parental responsibilities. So often do these appear in the major novels that they become a structural pattern. As the pattern recurs, it gives the novel cohesiveness, enabling Dickens to tie up his multiple plot threads and manipulate his gallery of characters.

In *David Copperfield,* for instance, the theme of the orphan and his surrogate parent affects all the major characters and interrelates them through David. After David is orphaned he enlarges his acquaintances by two other orphans, Little Emily and Ham, and their surrogate parent, Mr. Peggotty. To their home he unwittingly brings tragedy by introducing Steerforth, a demi-orphan. After finding refuge with Aunt Betsey, his surrogate mother, David adds three more half-orphans to his circle: Agnes Wickfield, Uriah Heep, and Annie Strong. His first marriage brings in yet another orphan, Dora Spenlow. Heep, through his meddling in the domestic affairs of the Strongs, his maneuvering to win Agnes, and his scheming to defraud her father and other victims, including Aunt Betsey, is finally brought to justice by another orphan, Tommy Traddles. Because David has been closely associated with all the principals, he is properly the one to report their final disposition. None are forgotten: Steerforth and Ham, who drown together; Emily, occupied with good works in Australia; Uriah, in prison, still falsely 'umble; and Agnes, whose happy life fulfills the deathbed promise made to Dora. With David and Agnes married, the theme of the orphan in search of identity and security is neatly resolved.

When the prevailing pattern is parental mistreatment of children, as in *Dombey and Son,* Dickens uses it effectively to control the plot. Thus Dombey, initially ignoring, then rejecting, his daughter while he pins his hopes on young Paul, denying him his childhood in the rush to advance him to a business partnership, loses both son and fortune. Throughout the novel it is Florence's devotion to her father, a love that demands nothing in return, that holds the plot together and is climaxed at last by Dombey's regeneration.

In those novels where parents have misguided and corrupted their children, there is cohesiveness because the major disasters are directly traceable to this travesty of home training. Jonas Chuzzlewit tries to poison the father who has taught him to be sly and self-seeking; then, thinking he has succeeded, he commits murder to escape detection, only to have the law close in on him, forcing him, ironically, to poison himself. Proud Mrs. Steerforth *(DC)* is reduced to imbecilic mutterings and painful periods of reliving the shock of her son's death, aware in her more lucid moments of her own part in his selfish arrogance. Gradgrind *(HT)* garners the fruits of his system in its disastrous impact on his own children.

Of the novels prominently employing parent-child inversion, *Little Dorrit* illustrates best how this pattern regulates the development of plot. As the little mother who zealously watches over her father in the Marshalsea, patiently putting up with his childish petulance and unfailingly supplying all his wants, Amy dominates the first half of the book. This maternal role she relinquishes temporarily when Dorrit comes into a fortune and takes his family to Italy, only to resume it when he collapses and lies dying. Thereafter Arthur Clennam, who has always thought of Amy as a child, takes over as a father figure. But, although he is far removed from the self-engrossed Dorrit, Amy mothers him as she tries to dispel his loneliness and ease his imprisonment by attending to his daily needs, just as she had done for her father. With this repetition of her maternal role in the Marshalsea, the plot has come full circle. After Clennam has regained his freedom and at last sees Amy for what she is, a mature woman who has loved him long, it requires only a brief conclusion to unite the two. A happy bride at last, the little mother has opened a new future for a once dispirited and hopeless man. Thus, in her inverted-mother role, Little Dorrit has given centrality to this novel.

The recurring patterns of the parent-child relationship may also interact with each other in a single novel, as they do in *David Copperfield*. As already indicated, David dominates the orphan-surrogate-parent theme. At the same time, as a friend of Steerforth and an enemy of Uriah, he is also involved in another chain of events that enable him to observe how two misguided mothers corrupt their sons. Finally, through his developing relationship with Agnes, he is virtually a party to the pattern of inverted parenthood as she mothers Mr. Wickfield. He further observes yet another inversion as Mrs. Markleham exploits her daughter, Annie Strong, for the sake of her own pampered existence. It is significant that Dickens has reserved for his favorite novel a combination of interacting patterns rather than a single pattern.

A fusion of art and social criticism, the recurring patterns of parent-child relations function metaphorically to anatomize nineteenth-century England. As Graham Smith has observed, "Dickens seizes upon the temporal and transmutes it into the material of underlying art."[8] Nowhere is this more apparent than in his treatment of the parent-child theme. His persistent use of this theme, moreover, is, as Steven Marcus has pointed out, "one of the clearest and most important indications of [his] continuing growth as a novelist."[9]

Although the current trend toward the novel of social protest aided Dickens's initial reception, his own campaign in behalf of the neglected, abused, and exploited child was by far the most vigorous of his century. It was also the most effective. Once public conscience was aroused, certain abuses became intolerable. After *Nicholas Nickleby*, for example, the notorious Yorkshire schools had to close because no one dared face the odium of patronizing such places.

Once Dickens had begun to identify negligent parents with the national social and political malaise, his warnings became more strident. He put society on trial and convicted it of ignoring its abandoned children, such as Jo the crossing sweeper *(BH)*. Again it must be emphasized that the darkening of his total vision reflected in part an uneasiness over his personal troubles and his problems with his own family.

But through it all Dickens never lost his ability to look at life from a child's point of view. His creativity demanded the imagination, the enthusiasm, the gaiety he derived from children. At first he took his stimulation from his own children when they were small. As they grew older, however, and he sensed an ever-widening gap between himself and them, he turned inward for inspiration, to the image of the twelve-year-old boy who had known the worst London slums, who had endured hunger and loneliness and humiliation. Here he found the world of his fiction, to be populated by children more real than those of his flesh.

Through his fictional children and their families he sustained his crusade and delivered his social creed: that the fate of a nation is inextricably linked with the survival of the home, that a benevolent state must step in where the home has not fulfilled its function. Children must be trained and made part of a nation's "glory, not its shame"; they must be a token of its "strength, not its weakness." The amplification of these simple convictions justified the confidence Dickens expressed in his will: "I rest my claim to the remembrance of my country upon my published work."

Because, like that small company of the greatest literary figures, Dickens was "not of an age but for all time," his insistence on improved parent-child relations is as relevant today as in the nineteenth century. In a period when the family has begun to disintegrate, when more children are the victims of broken homes and parental neglect, when an acquisitive society is often indifferent to the loss of moral fiber in its young, his fears for the future of the state are as pertinent as ever. Selfish parents, alienated and lonely children, indifferent and calloused officials—all are still with us. The efforts of social workers and the expenditures of charitable and public offices notwithstanding, many children are still homeless, undernourished, abused. Others, even in affluent homes, feel rejected, misunderstood, abandoned because their parents, preoccupied with social and material aspirations, have ignored basic family needs. Too often parental permissiveness has been the easier alternative to disciplined training and character building. With their homes no longer giving centrality to their lives, many young people, rejecting the values of their middle-class background, have developed a nomadic subculture. Drug addiction, violence, destructiveness—these set them apart from structured society. Their homes spiritually bankrupt, church and state seemingly indifferent to their personal problems, the young have repudiated their elders' mores. At its best the situation may be viewed as a generation gap; at its worst, as anarchy.

Yet the young are not solely responsible for their alienation from constituted authority. Too many have been denied the right to work, to maintain their self-esteem through meaningful productivity. Like the inmates of the nineteenth-century workhouses, "pleasantly so-named, because work cannot be done in them," as Carlyle observed, they are dispirited, "their hopes, outlooks, share of the fair world" denied them (*Past and Present*, I, 1). Bored by their meaningless existence, exasperated by the futility of seeking work, despondent over the bleaknesss of their future, they either resort to noisy and destructive demonstrations or withdraw into despair—even into the ultimate withdrawal, suicide. All this because of a missing ingredient, love—love between child and parent or between the child and the state *in loco parentis.* "Without love men cannot endure to be together," Carlyle warned (*Past and Present*, IV, 4). Love was the remedy which Dickens prescribed to ensure "better homes when [children are] a-lying in [their] cradles." So today, as family disintegration threatens our national security, his prescription still holds the only promise of survival. Never have his books spoken more persuasively than today. Their continuing plea ensures his own expressed hope "that my books will speak for themselves and me, when I and my faults, my fortunes and misfortunes, are all forgotten."

Notes

Abbreviations used to identify manuscript and published sources:

Berg MS.   Letters in the Berg Collection of the New York Public Library
Br. Lib.   Letters from Katey Dickens Perugini to George Bernard Shaw in the British Library Department of Manuscripts
Fields Papers   Letters and Diaries of Annie Fields (Mrs. James T.) in the Massachusetts Historical Society Library, Boston
Hunt. MS.   Letters in the Henry E. Huntington Library and Art Gallery, San Marino, California
House MS.   Letters in the Humphry E. House Collection, Cambridge, England
Morgan MS.   Letters in the Pierpont Morgan Library, New York
Nonesuch   *The Nonesuch Edition of the Letters of Charles Dickens*, 3 vols. Edited by Walter Dexter. London: Nonesuch Press, 1938.
Ouvry Papers   Letters relating to Frederic Ouvry's association with members of the Dickens family; owned by Sir Leslie Farrer, K. C. V. O., London
Pilgrim   *The Pilgrim Edition of the Letters of Charles Dickens*, 5 vols. to date. Edited by Madeline House, Graham Storey, Kathleen Tillotson, and K. J. Fielding. Oxford: Clarendon Press, 1965, 1969, 1974, 1977, 1981.

CHAPTER 1

1. For an excellent historical summary of this discipline, see Grylls, *Guardians and Angels*, pp. 24–38; and Pattison, *The Child Figure in English Literature*, pp. 19–30.

2. Thomas Arnold to G. Cornish, quoted by Stanley in *Life and Correspondence of Dr. Arnold* 1:161.

3. G. R. Sims, *How the Poor Live*, quoted by Devas, *Studies in Family Life*, p. 261.

4. C. Dickens to T. J. Thompson, 29 April 1844, *Pilgrim* IV: 89.

5. See Grylls, *Guardians and Angels,* pp. 28–38.

CHAPTER 2

1. Although I have found no local newspaper reference to this second evening of dancing, both Hesketh Pearson (*Dickens, His Character, Comedy, and Career,* p. 1) and Edgar Johnson (*Charles Dickens: His Tragedy and Triumph,* p. 9) state that Elizabeth Dickens, accompanied by her husband, attended a party on the evening preceding her confinement and danced vigorously.

2. Wilson, *The World of Charles Dickens,* p. 290.

3. These were Dickens's own impressions as recalled later in "An Unsettled Neighbourhood" (*HW,* 11 November 1854). See also his speech at the anniversary dinner of University College Hospital, 12 April 1864, in Fielding, *The Speeches of Charles Dickens,* p. 326.

4. T. Wemyss Reid, "The Rambling Philosopher," as quoted in the Bolton *Guardian,* 10 October 1887.

5. C. Dickens to W. Irving, 21 April 1841, *Pilgrim* 2:268.

6. Angus Easson, *Dickensian* 70 (January 1974): 39.

7. C. Dickens to J. Forster, [June 1862], *Nonesuch* 3:297.

8. Kitton, *Charles Dickens by Pen and Pencil* 1: 9–10.

9. Forster, *Life,* Ley ed., p. 35.

CHAPTER 3

1. M. Dickens, "Charles Dickens at Home," p. 33.

2. C. Dickens to Catherine Dickens, 4 November 1853, *Nonesuch* 2:507.

3. M. Dickens, "Charles Dickens at Home," p. 33.

4. C. Dickens to H. Austin, 25 September 1842, *Pilgrim* 3:331.

5. C. Dickens to M. Dickens, 27 February 1849, *Nonesuch* 2:147.

6. M. Dickens, *My Father as I Recall Him,* p. 38.

7. Ibid., p. 39.

8. C. Dickens, Jr. "Glimpses of Charles Dickens," pp. 523–26.

9. Quoted by M. Dickens, *My Father as I Recall Him,* p. 38. This quotation appears verbatim in stave 3 of *A Christmas Carol.*

10. Ibid., p. 23.

11. Ibid., p. 46.

12. C. Dickens, Jr., "Glimpses of Charles Dickens," p. 527.

13. C. Dickens to Angela Burdett-Coutts, 27 December 1843, in Johnson, *Heart of Charles Dickens,* p. 59.

14. Quoted by H. Dickens, *Recollections,* p. 40.

15. C. Dickens to Catherine Dickens, 23 November 1844, *Pilgrim* 4:-229.

16. M. Dickens, *My Father as I Recall Him,* pp. 25–26.

17. H. Dickens, *Recollections,* pp. 26–27.

18. C. Dickens to Angela Burdett-Coutts, 5 July 1856, in Johnson, *Heart of Charles Dickens,* p. 320.

19. H. Dickens, *Memories of My Father,* pp. 25–26, and *Recollections,* p. 21.

20. M. A. Dickens, "A Child's Memories," p. 73.

21. Quoted by M. Dickens, "Charles Dickens at Home," p. 37.

22. M. Dickens, *My Father as I Recall Him,* p. 13.

23. Ritchie, "Charles Dickens as I Remember Him," pp. 308–9.

24. C. Dickens to W. Brackenbury, 18 September 1865, House MS.

25. C. Dickens to Angela Burdett-Coutts, 7 August 1843, *Pilgrim* 3:-539.

26. C. Dickens to Mrs. Godfrey, 25 July 1839, *Pilgrim* 1:567; and C. Dickens to S. R. Starey, 24 September 1843, *Pilgrim* 3:574.

27. Quoted in H. Dickens, *Recollections,* pp. 41–42.

28. C. Dickens to Angela Burdett-Coutts, 14 January 1854, in Johnson, *Heart of Charles Dickens,* p. 254.

29. H. James to Alice James, 10 March 1869, in *The Letters of Henry James,* 5 vols. Edited by Leon Edel. Boston: Harvard University Press, 1974—1:16.

30. H. Dickens, *Recollections,* p. 95. For an account of Lynch see Adrian, *Georgina Hogarth and the Dickens Circle,* pp. 127 and 132.

31. M. Dickens, *My Father as I Recall Him,* p. 2.

32. M. Dickens to A. Fields, 1 September 1870, Hunt. MS. Quoted in Adrian, *Georgina Hogarth,* p. 158.

33. Carlton, "Dickens Family Links with Fenton," p. 10.

34. Storey, *Dickens and Daughter,* p. 177.

35. H. James to Alice James, 10 March 1869, *Letters of Henry James* 1:16.

36. Information supplied by the late Henry Charles Dickens in an interview.

37. M. Dickens, *My Father as I Recall Him,* p. 10.

38. Storey, *Dickens and Daughter,* p. 106.

39. Ibid., p. 134.

40. Ibid., p. 91.

41. At Shaw's suggestion these letters were given to the British Museum. Katey's letters to Shaw are in the Manuscript Room of the British Library: ADD MS. 50546.

42. C. Dickens to Angela Burdett-Coutts, 22 August 1851, in Johnson, *Heart of Charles Dickens,* p. 187.

43. C. Dickens to Georgina Hogarth, 12 October 1864, Hunt. MS. Quoted in Adrian, *Georgina Hogarth,* p. 86.

44. For a more detailed account of Alfred's debts see Adrian, *Georgina Hogarth,* p. 88.

45. Information supplied by the late Henry Charles Dickens in an interview.

46. C. Dickens to Catherine Dickens, 3 September 1850, *Nonesuch* 2:642.

47. S. Dickens to C. Dickens, 19 March 1869, Ouvry Papers. Quoted in Adrian, *Georgina Hogarth,* p. 123.

48. C. Dickens to E. M. Winter, 12 March 1855, *Nonesuch* 2:642.

49. C. Dickens to C. Fechter [September 1968], *Nonesuch* 3:669.

50. Br. Lib., ADD MS. 50446.

51. C. Dickens to H. Dickens, 15 October 1868, *Nonesuch* 3:673.

52. H. Dickens, *Memories of My Father,* pp. 19–20.

53. C. Dickens to E. M. Winter, 22 February 1855, *Nonesuch* 2:633.

54. H. Dickens, *Memories of My Father,* p. 19.

55. C. Dickens to W. Macready, 27 December 1869, Morgan MS.

56. C. Dickens to E. Dickens [26 September 1868], *Nonesuch* 3:668.

57. C. Dickens to Angela Burdett-Coutts, 3 January 1854, Johnson, *Heart of Charles Dickens,* p. 251.

58. Ginott, *Between Parent and Child,* p. 37.

59. Bartemeier, "The Contribution of the Father," pp. 277–80.

60. H. Dickens, *Memories of My Father,* p. 26.

61. C. Dickens to W. Collins, 17 July 1856, *Nonesuch* 2:680.

62. Ibid., 3:360.

63. C. Dickens to George Dolby, 25 September 1868, Berg. MS.

64. C. Dickens to Mrs. Gore, 17 September 1852, *Nonesuch* 2:416.

65. Orr, "Charles Dickens as Husband," pp. 14–17.

66. C. Dickens to Wills, 6 June 1867, Hunt. MS. Quoted in Adrian, *Georgina Hogarth,* p. 158.

67. C. Dickens to W. Collins, 4 October 1866, *Nonesuch* 3:487.

68. Fields Papers, 23 February 1870. Quoted in Adrian, *Georgina Hogarth,* p. 158.

69. Br. Lib., ADD MS., 50546.

70. Lazarus, *A Tale of Two Brothers,* p. 110.

71. Ginott, *Between Parent and Child,* p. 37.

72. C. Dickens to J. Forster, April 1846, *Nonesuch* 2:765.

73. Lehmann, *Ancestors and Friends,* p. 211. The year given is 1864.

74. See Fielding, "Charles Dickens and His Wife," p. 216.

75. Byrne, *Gossip of the Century,* pp. 255–57.
76. Br. Lib. ADD Ms., 50446.

CHAPTER 4

1. Sackville-West, "Dickens and the World of Childhood," p. 22.
2. M. Dickens, quoted by Kitton, *Charles Dickens by Pen and Pencil,* Supplement, p. 47.
3. C. Dickens to T. Mitton, 4 April 1842, *Pilgrim,* 3:191.
4. Ibid., [20 November 1834], 1:44.
5. Johnson, *Charles Dickens* 1:258.
6. C. Dickens to J. Forster [11 July 1839], *Pilgrim, 1:560.*
7. C. Dickens to T. Mitton, 28 September 1843, ibid., 3:375.
8. C. Dickens to T. Mitton, 14 February 1844, ibid. 4:45.
9. Forster, *Life,* p. 538.
10. For an account of Augustus's Chicago family and Dickens's refusal to recognize this connection, see Moss, "Dickens and His Chicago Relatives," pp. 22–28.
11. Dickens, Jr., "Glimpses of Charles Dickens," p. 683.
12. C. Dickens to G. Beadnell, 19 December 1838, *Pilgrim* 1:620.

CHAPTER 5

1. For a discussion of Fagin as the devil and his London as hell, see Lauriat Lane, Jr., "The Devil in *Oliver Twist,*" *Dickensian* 52 (1956): 14.
2. Michael Slater, "On Reading *Oliver Twist,*" *Dickensian* 70 (1974): 78. For an earlier treatment of Fagin's momentary tenderness toward Oliver, see Arthur A. Adrian, "Charles Dickens: A Twentieth-Century Postmortem," *Victorians Institute Journal* 1 (1972): 13.
3. See Tillotson, *Novels of the Eighteen-Forties,* p. 30.
4. Leavis and Leavis, *Dickens: The Novelist,* p. 94.
5. Stange, "Expectations Well Lost: Dickens' Fable for His Time," p. 14.
6. See Dessner, *"Great Expectations:* 'the ghost of a man's own father.'" Using a "psychoanalytic reading" to arrive at "a unified explanation of the novel's central meaning and of the incongruities between the novel and received critical accounts of it," Dessner argues that Magwitch, not Joe, is the father figure who will "love and punish Pip" and also "redeem his burden of guilt by punishing him."

CHAPTER 6

1. Jerome Meckier, "Dickens in *King Lear:* A Myth for Victorian England," *South Atlantic Quarterly* 71(Winter 1972):70–90.

CHAPTER 9

1. See Rooke's "Fathers and Sons in Dickens," pp. 53–69.

2. Ibid. See also Levin's "The Uncles in Dickens."

3. Dickens often expressed his dissatisfaction with the English state and church, and especially the "do-nothing" aristocracy. See his letter to Forster [March 1844], *Pilgrim* 3:74; and Douglas Jerrold, 3 May 1843, *Pilgrim* 3:482.

4. In the Eastgate House Museum, Rochester, England, an index to press cuttings and other materials relating to Dickens includes an entry entitled "Mrs. Dickens' secret visit to Gad's Hill." It is described as a letter by W. Roberts. The cutting itself is, unfortunately, missing. The item is numbered 324 + +.

5. "I have had stern occasion to impress upon my children that their father's name is their best possession ... ," C. Dickens to F. M. Evans, 22 August 1858, *Nonesuch* 3:33.

6. C. Dickens, "Where We Stopped Growing," *Household Words*, 1 January 1853.

7. Jean Jacques Rousseau, *Émile*. Trans. William Boyd. New York: Teachers College Press, 1960.

8. Smith, *Dickens, Money, and Society*, p. 51.

9. Marcus, *Dickens: From Pickwick to Dombey*, p. 43.

A Select Bibliography

BIOGRAPHY AND CRITICISM

Adrian, Arthur A. *Georgina Hogarth and the Dickens Circle*. London and New York: Oxford University Press, 1957.

Axton, William F. *A Circle of Fire: Dickens' Vision and Style and the Popular Victorian Theater*. Lexington: University of Kentucky Press, 1966.

Bayley, John. "Oliver Twist: Things as They Really Are." In *Dickens and the Twentieth Century*. Toronto: University of Toronto Press, 1962.

Bell, Vernon M. "Parents and Children in *Great Expectations*." *Victorian Newsletter* (Spring 1965):21–24.

Brown, Ivor. *Dickens in His Time*. London: Thomas Nelson and Sons, 1963.

Butt, John I., and Kathleen Tillotson. *Dickens at Work*. London: Methuen, 1957.

Carey, John. *The Violent Effigy: A Study of Dickens' Imagination*. London: Faber, 1973.

Carlton, William J. "Dickens Family Links with Fenton." Andover *Advertiser*, 25 July 1969, p. 10.

Christie, Octavius F. *Dickens and His Age*. London: Heath Cranton, Ltd., 1939.

Coburn, Lloyd Paul. "Charles Dickens: Parent-Child Relationships." Ph. D. dissertation, Case Western Reserve University, 1956.

Cockshut, Anthony O. J. *The Imagination of Charles Dickens*. London: Collins, 1961.

Collins, Philip. *Dickens and Crime*. New York: St. Martin's Press, 1962.

———. *Dickens and Education*. London: Macmillan, 1963.

———. editor. *Dickens, the Critical Heritage*. New York: Barnes & Noble, Inc., 1971.

Coveney, Peter. *Poor Monkey, the Child in Literature*. London, Rockliff, 1957.

Davis, Earle. *The Flint and the Flame: The Artistry of Charles Dickens*. Columbia, Mo.: University of Missouri Press, 1963.

Dessner, Lawrence J. "*Great Expectations:* 'the ghost of a man's own Father.'" *PMLA*, 91 (May 1975):436–49.

Dickens, Charles, Jr. "Glimpses of Charles Dickens." *North American Review* 109 (May, June 1895): 523–37, 677–84.

Dickens, Charles, III. "My Grandfather at Christmas-time." *The Girl's Own Annual* 30 (December 1908): 109–111.

Dickens, Sir Henry F. *Memories of My Father.* London: V. Gollanz, Ltd., 1928.

———. *Recollections of Sir Henry Dickens.* London: Heinemann, 1934.

Dickens, Mary. *Charles Dickens, by his eldest daughter.* London: Cassell & Co., 1885.

———. "Charles Dickens at Home." *The Cornhill Magazine,* new series 4 (January 1885): 32–51.

———. *My Father as I Recall Him.* New York: Dutton, 1897.

Dickens, Mary Angela. "A Child's Recollections of Gad's Hill." *The Strand Magazine* 12 (January 1897): 60–74.

Donoghue, Denis. "The English Dickens and *Dombey and Son.*" In *Dickens Centennial Essays.* Edited by Ada Nisbet and Blake Nevius. Berkeley: University of California Press, 1971.

Dyson, A. E. *The Inimitable Dickens.* London: Macmillan, 1970.

Fielding, K. J. *Charles Dickens: A Critical Introduction,* 2d ed. London: Longmans, 1963.

———. "Charles Dickens and His Wife: Fact or Forgery?" *Études Anglaises* 8 (July-December 1955): 212–22.

———, ed. *The Speeches of Charles Dickens.* Oxford: Clarendon Press, 1960.

Ford, George H. Introduction to the Riverside edition of *David Copperfield.* Boston: Houston Mifflin Co., 1958.

———, and Lauriat Lane, Jr., eds. *The Dickens Critics.* Ithaca: Cornell University Press, 1961.

Forster, John. *The Life of Charles Dickens.* Edited and annotated with an introduction by J. W. T. Ley. New York: Doubleday Doran, 1928.

Gold, Joseph. *Charles Dickens: Radical Moralist.* Minneapolis: University of Minnesota Press, 1972.

Grylls, David. *Guardians and Angels: Parents and Children in Nineteenth-Century Literature.* London and Boston: Faber & Faber, 1978.

Hardwick, John Michael, and Mollie Hardwick. *As They Saw Him: Charles Dickens.* London: George G. Harrap & Co., Ltd., 1970.

Hardy, Barbara. *Charles Dickens: The Later Novels.* London: Longmans, 1928.

Healey, Edna. *Lady Unknown: The Life of Angela Burdett-Coutts.* London: Sedgwick & Jackson, 1978.

Herbert, Christopher. "De Quincey and Dickens." *Victorian Studies* 17 (March 1974): 248–60.

Hill, Nancy K. *A Reformer's Art: Dickens' Picturesque and Grotesque Imagery.* Athens and London: Ohio University Press, 1981.

Johnson, Edgar. *Charles Dickens: His Tragedy and Triumph,* 2 vols. New York: Simon and Schuster, 1952.

———, ed. *The Heart of Charles Dickens. As Revealed in His Letters to Angela Burdett-Coutts.* New York: Duell, Sloan and Pearce, 1952.

Johnson, E. D. H. *Charles Dickens: An Introduction to His Novels.* New York: Random House, 1967.

Kincaid, James R. *Dickens and the Rhetoric of Laughter.* Oxford: Clarendon Press, 1971.

Kitton, Frederic G. *Charles Dickens by Pen and Pencil.* Supplement. London: T. Sabin, 1890.

Lane, Margaret. *Purely for Pleasure.* New York: Alfred A. Knopf, 1967.

Lazarus Mary. *A Tale of Two Brothers.* Sydney: Angus and Robertson, 1973.

Leavis, F. R., and Q. D. Leavis. *Dickens: The Novelist.* London: Chatto and Windus, 1970.

Levin, Harry. "The Uncles in Dickens." In *The Worlds of Charles Dickens.* Cambridge, Mass.: Harvard University Press, 1975.

Lindsay, Jack. *Charles Dickens: A Biographical and Critical Study.* London: Dakers, 1950.

Mackenzie, Norman I., and Jeanne D. Mackenzie. *Dickens, a Life.* Oxford and New York: Clarendon Press, 1979.

Manning, Sylvia B. *Dickens as Satirist.* New Haven: Yale University Press, 1971.

———. "Masking and Self-Revelation: Dickens's Three Autobiographies." *Dickens Studies Newsletter* 7 (September 1976): 69–75.

Marcus, Steven. *Dickens: From Pickwick to Dombey.* New York: Basic Books, 1965.

Matchett, Willoughby. "Dickens in Bayham Street." *Dickensian* 5 (June, July 1909): 147–52, 180–84.

Miller, J. Hillis. *Charles Dickens: The World of His Novels.* Cambridge, Mass.: Harvard University Press, 1958.

Milner, Ian. "The Dickens Drama: Mr. Dombey." In *Dickens Centennial Essays.* Edited by Nisbet and Nevius. Berkeley: University of California Press, 1971.

Monod, Sylvère. *Dickens Romancier.* Paris: Hatchette, 1953.

Moss, Sidney P. "Dickens and His Chicago Relatives." *Dickensian* 78 (Spring 1982): 22–28.

Newman, S. J. *Dickens at Play.* London: Macmillan, 1981.

Nisbet, Ada. *Dickens and Ellen Ternan.* Berkeley: University of California Press, 1971.

Orr, Lyndon. "Charles Dickens as Husband." *Bookman* (New York) 23 (March 1906): 14–17.

Pattison, Robert. *The Child Figure in English Literature.* Athens: University of Georgia Press, 1978.

Perugini, Katey Dickens, "My Father's Love of Children." *Dickensian* 7 (May 1911): 117–19.

Ritchie, Anne Thackeray. "Charles Dickens as I Remember Him." *Pall Mall Magazine* 49 (March 1912): 301–9.

Rooke, Eleanor. "Fathers and Sons in Dickens." In *Essays and Studies* (1951). Edited for the English Association by Geoffrey Tillotson.

Sackville-West, Edward. "Dickens and the World of Childhood." In *Inclinations.* London: Secker and Warburg, 1949.

Sandford, A. E. "Aspects of Parents and Children in the Novels of Charles Dickens." M. Litt. dissertation, University of Edinburgh, 1968.

Smith, Graham. *Dickens, Money, and Society.* Berkeley: University of California Press. 1968.

Spilka, Mark. *Dickens and Kafka: A Mutual Interpretation.* Bloomington: Indiana University Press, 1963.

Stange, Robert, "Expectations Well Lost: Dickens' Fable for His Time." *College English* 16 (L954): 9–17.

Stoehr, Taylor. *Dickens: The Dreamer's Stance.* Ithaca: Cornell University Press, 1965.

Stone, Harry. "Dark Corners in the Mind: Dickens's Childhood Reading." *Horn Book Magazine,* June 1963.

Storey, Gladys. *Dickens and Daughter.* New York: Haskell, 1971. Originally published by F. Miller, 1939.

Tillotson, Kathleen. *Novels of the Eighteen-Forties.* Oxford: Clarendon Press, 1954.

_____. Introduction to *Oliver Twist,* the Clarendon Dickens Series. Oxford, 1966.

Trilling, Lionel. "Little Dorrit." In *The Opposing Self.* New York: Viking, 1955.

Wilson, Angus. "Dickens on Children and Childhood." In *Dickens 1970.* Edited by Michael Slater. London: Chapman and Hall, 1970.

_____. *The World of Charles Dickens.* London: Martin Secker & Warburg, 1970.

Wilson, Edmund. "Dickens: The Two Scrooges." In *The Wound and the Bow; Seven Studies in Literature.* Boston: Houghton Mifflin, 1941.

Worth, George. *Dickensian Melodrama: A Reading of the Novels.* Lawrence: University of Kansas Press, 1978.

Zabel, Morton. Introduction to the Riverside edition of *Bleak House.* Boston: Houghton Mifflin, 1956.

_____. "The Revolutionary Fate." In *Craft and Character in Modern Fiction.* New York: Viking, 1957.

MEMOIRS AND SOCIAL HISTORY

Altick, Richard D. *Victorian People and Ideas.* New York: Norton, 1973.

Ariès, Philippe. *Centuries of Childhood. A Social History of Family Life.* Translated by Robert Baldick. New York: Alfred A. Knopf, 1962.

Avery, Gillian. *The Echoing Green: Memories of Victorian Youth.* New York: Viking, 1974.

_____. *Nineteenth-Century Children.* London: Hodder and Stoughton, 1965.

_____. *Victorian People in Life and Literature.* New York: Holt, Rinehart & Winston, 1970.

Beames, Thomas. *The Rookeries of London.* London: Thomas Bosworth, 1850.

Burton, Elizabeth. *The Early Victorians at Home.* London: Longmans, 1972.

Byrne, Julia C. B. *Gossip of the Century.* London: Ward & Downey, 1882.

Culmer, W. H. *Billy the Cartwheeler: "The Last of the Dickens Boys."* Metuchen, N. J.: Scarecrow Press, 1970.

Dunlop, Olive Jocelyn, and Richard D. Denman. *English Apprenticeship and Child Labour: A History.* London: T. F. Unwin, 1912; New York: Macmillan, 1976.

Foakes-Jackson, Frederick John. *Social Life in England, 1750–1850.* New York: Macmillan, 1916.

Greenwood, James. *The Seven Curses of London.* Boston: S. Rivers & Co., 1869.

_____. *The Wilds of London.* London: Guildford, 1874.

Hare, Augustus. *The Story of My Life.* New York: Dodd, Mead & Co., 1896–1901.

Kellett, E. *Religion and Life in the Early Victorian Age.* London: Epworth Press, 1938.

Lehmann, John Frederick. *Ancestors and Friends.* London: Eyre & Spottiswoode, 1962.

Mayhew, Henry. *London Labour and the London Poor,* 5 vols. New York: A. M. Kelley, 1967.

Morrison, Arthur. *A Child of the Jago.* Chicago: A. S. Stone & Co., 1906.

_____. *Tales of Mean Streets.* London: Methuen, 1894.

Reader, William J. *Life in Victorian England.* London: B. T. Batsford, 1965.

Roe, F. Gordon. *The Victorian Child.* London: Phoenix House, 1959.

Stanley, Arthur P. *The Life and Correspondence of Thomas Arnold,* 2 vols. London: B. Fellows, 1844.

Unstead, Robert John. *Looking at History.* London: A. & C. Black, 1955.

STUDIES OF THE CHILD AND THE FAMILY

Bartemeier, Leo. "The Contribution of the Father to the Mental Health of the Family." *American Journal of Psychology* 110 (October 1853), 277–80.
Devas, C. S. *Studies in Family Life.* London: Burns and Oates, 1886.
Gesell, Arnold F., and Francis L. Gesell. *The Child from Five to Ten.* New York: Harper & Bros., 1946.
Ginott, Haim. *Between Parent and Child.* New York: Macmillan, 1965.
Greene, Graham. *The Lost Childhood and Other Essays.* New York: Viking, 1951.

PSYCHOLOGICAL STUDIES

Brain, Russell. *Some Reflections on Genius.* New York: Pitnam Medical Publishing Co., 1960.
Brussell, James A. "Charles Dickens: Child Psychologist and Sociologist" Pt. 1. *Psychiatric Quarterly Supplement,* 1938.
"The Law as Father." *The American Imago* 12 (Spring 1955): 17–23.
Manheim, Leonard F. *The Dickens Pattern: A Study of Psychoanalytic Creation.* Ann Arbor: University Microfilms, 1950.
"The Personal History of David Copperfield: A Study of Psychoanalytic Criticism." *The American Imago* 9 (1953): 31–43.
Superstein, Milton R. *Emotional Security.* New York: Crown Publishers, 1948.

Index